CLOUDS AND RAIN

A China-to-America Memoir

EDNA WU

EVANSTON PUBLISHING, INC.
EVANSTON, ILLINOIS 60201

This is a fictional memoir. Its characters, places, and incidents are either fictional or used fictitiously, and their resemblance, if any, to real-life counterparts is entirely coincidental. Any reference to historical events, to real people, living or dead, or to real locales are intended only to give the work a sense of reality and authenticity.

Acknowledgement

Joseph Brodsky's poem "New Life," from which I quoted two lines, was translated by David MacFadyen and the author and first published in *The New Yorker*, April 26,1993. The two poems by Mei and "The Family Tree" in the novel were written by my daughter Lin Jin. Among my own poems, "Chinese Love," "At Clarion Cemetery," "Birch" appeared in *The Pen* (The PBC, Newport News); "Follow Me" in *Lines and Ribbons* (*Lavender Letter*); and "Nothing but a Kite" in *Collages and Bricolages* (Clarion). Several of my other poems, which first appeared in anthologies or other poetic collections, have been used in this novel in their revised form. I thank Terry Caesar and other readers for their comments on the early draft of the novel.

Chinese calligraphy by Yuanchong Hwang.

EVANSTON PUBLISHING, INC.
1571 SHERMAN AVE., ANNEX C
EVANSTON, IL 60201

Printed in the U.S.A.

Library of Congress Card Catalog Number: 93-73542

ISBN 1-879260-22-0

In the new life, a cloud is better than the bright sun.
The rain, akin to self-knowledge, appears perpetual.
                                                — Joseph Brodsky

To Love

A Skyscraper

On the debris of the guttural ruins
rises the modern Babel
boasts of dribbling the ball of meta-reality
in a labial model
but scrapes from the sky
nothing but air
in the sunlight
remains indeed
a Block
with a phoenix trail of
shadow
--
=
.

Searching for the Music of the Soul

After a few weeks of tears and pain, I finally killed the angel of love in me and was able to reconstruct this damned funny book. Really, I have no talent for writing. Sometimes, I stood aside, trying to view myself as a cool outsider; but most of the time I simply threw in fragments of my diary.

ϕ ❦ ❦ ❦ ❦

That day Yun was taken with Ramon during their first conversation. Since she often declared herself to be a living Romanticist, she felt she could not be attacked by anything but an emotional intensity. Luckily, she drove home without having an accident, though the shining paint was scratched along the car's left shoulder by her yard stone. The intensity paralyzed her and sent her to bed, curling like a shivering kitten. She called "Ra—mon, Ra—mon. . ." with a longing and passion that surpassed Rochester's calling for Jane. The sexuality of her long-numbed body started to revive. She felt the tightening of her bra and a thrill shot up from the deep red valley, radiating through and through. Nothing could help relieve such an intensity, except an auto-erotic release.

When she became tranquil, she walked aside from herself, re-seeing the videotape of her behavior in a flashback. She became meditative. In the contact between a man and a woman, sexual sensitivity is always alive, embering or flaming. Is it possible to see a man and a woman simply as asexual beings?

She sat up, reflecting upon her own stereotypes of sexual differences: a man seems to be attracted more by the appearance and body of the opposite sex, while a woman is likely to be magnetized more by soul and intelligence. A man desires a woman to be virtuous and nurturing like a mother and he is content to live with a woman who is intellectually dull; yet a woman can hardly be content with a partner who performs well merely as a good nurse or housekeeper.

Yes, her and her husband's sexual roles have been reversed since, or even before their marriage. She has been the president, ambassador, legislator of the house, while her husband does household chores, such as cooking, shopping, cleaning, and gardening. If she were really a man, she would be content to enjoy the banality of a happy life. Yet she is in pain all the time. She longs more for intellectual communication than for daily food and a comfortable bed. Her emotions, which have never been aroused even once by her husband, are deadened by a life without windows.

❦ ❦ ❦ ❦ ❦

> *Life is almost perfect for me*
> *but that nobody shares the music of my soul*
> *He is lofty as is he tall*
> *A handsome portrait—*
> *To behold his height*
> *one must step away*
>
> *Yes, I must be in love with a man*
> *so deep that I have no words to say*
> *so intelligently that I am*
> *unwilling to say*
> *The permissible handshake conveys so much—*
> *so little.*

❦ ❦ ❦ ❦ ❦

Ramon is Mexican-American, with a Mexican wife and two big boys. The night she met him happened to be the first day of the LA riots. A lot of buildings were being torched, much blood was flowing, the sprawling Land of Angels was splitting up. Are you horrified? Yes, I am. My heart aches for the nation. It must be set free from its racial ghettoization. People should be judged by their human qualities, not their skin color. Of course, the LA riot is not skin-deep. The skin camouflages a fierce struggle between power and human dignity, between money and poverty.

Yun was thinking about his calm comments. It was a fight

not only between the black and the white but also between the black and the yellow. A couple of Chinese, mistaken as Koreans, were killed in the riots. People now came to see a vicious circle: yesterday the black/the white; today the black/the yellow, tomorrow could be the brown/the yellow or among the yellows of different shades. Yun felt ashamed of her own race. She learned from Long that in many shops owned by the Chinese, Mexican employees did the hardest work but got the lowest pay. In turn, however, the Chinese suffered the same in stores owned by another race. She recalled how one night when she and her daughter Mei were taking an evening stroll, they met the parents of Mei's classmate Eric. Eric was the youngest of eight children in his family. His parents still looked young. Yun learned that most of the Chicano families in the neighborhood had four to eight kids. When she said having many kids would lower the standard of living, Eric's father laughed good-naturedly: "Having more kids is our political strategy. A couple of years ago, the Mexican community was seriously talking about taking back California through our biological power. We are becoming the majority in Los Angeles." Now Yun came to realize that quantity was not that important. To improve the social status of a race, each community needs people like Ramon, who had struggled to reap a PhD at Yale without forgetting his own roots.

The flaming buildings and the bloody violence transmitted by the TV intensified her love for Ramon. One moment she dreamt that Ramon went with her to visit China. The authority of the Wuhan University refused to give them an honorable banquet as they had for other visiting Americans. Yun knew it was simply because Ramon was a Mexican-American. Yun took Ramon to see her mother and sisters and brothers. All of them looked cold simply because he did not disguise his pure Mexican roots. If Yun came home with Bob, a man old enough to be her father, they might still look up to him because of his Anglo-Saxon complexion; if Yun came home with Philip, a hunchback, they might still feel accepting, because his Irish blood had overtaken his great-grandma's native Indian blood. Ramon was Yun's age, handsome and athletic, but she was forced to hide him in her handbag from her own people. Still she could hear the neighbors gossiping: A Mexican? Where is Mexico? Oh, I see, in Africa. Another moment, Prues and Karen appeared before her. They both advised her not to meddle in the life of another married man—wife, children, and family are sacred.

No! I do not intend to marry any man. I am not taking him away from any other woman. I am not destroying anybody or anything. But the soul, being colorless and raceless, belongs to the whole universe.

Among lofty mountain peaks and ceaseless flows of sea, a soul, seized by love, is composing the bosom music—an incomplete music of loneliness and isolation that is searching for a synchronizing rhythm from another soul, an understanding listener.

The intensity of thinking wrung tears from her heart. Love feels its deepest when it cannot be stopped by a despairing realization of an utter impossibility.

An image, a word evokes such paralyzing force. The wind asked her, "Where is a woman's center in love?"

Her heart was howling his name over the vast span of a dark ocean.

Even the impossibility is the bottomless sea, a bird picks up a straw or a pebble with her tiny red beak and drop it into the sea with a heart-rending call.

The mountain asked her, "Where is a woman's center in love?"

"Ra—mon, Ra—mon . . . Jingwei . . . Jing—wei—. . ."

The calling for the other gradually changed to a call for the self. The bird is called Jingwei, the myth says. She gathers her strength after each splash by chanting her own name.

Tears dried, she returned to work.

> *Words form mere icebergs above the sea.*
> *How could they convey the meaning beneath?*
> *Calmness on the chilly white surface*
> *disguises convulsive fire in ice.*

An iceberg hides its volcanoes just like the earth.

May 15

Love is not sex or marriage, but an emotional intensity—a fragmenting, paralyzing, and suicidal force.

I believe it is such an intensity that killed Sylvia Plath.

A creative intensity, parallel to the intensity of love, split Virginia Woolf's nerves.

Intensity is bliss, but also the last sting of the queen bee.

My mind is sprawling like a wild tree
unable to prune itself
My nerves are splitting in all directions
leaving a hollow center where a will used to be
I am thinking of him
Not him but his words
One needs something larger or higher than
oneself to drive
the boat of life
A political ideal, disillusioned
Love   failed
Nothing
but deadly boredom
Ennui. . . .

Before dawn Yun awoke from an erotic dream, her tears slipping out, washing her face. To get rid of her longing for Ramon, she had a shower and jogged in the morning glow.

Coming back, she wrote a cheerful, disinterested poem.

Dawn
Roosters sing to greet the birth of the sun.
Vibrating with aspiration,
Inspiration comes with foot-tapping on the dewy grass.

Dawn
Flowers crane their necks to suck fresh air.
Renewed by a morning shower,
The poise of nature defies red dust.

Dawn
Flocks of birds vie to offer their opinions.
True democracy
will never outstep the door of Nature.

Mei got up and asked her what she was doing. She started teaching Mei the form of a sixteen-syllable poem she had just written in Chinese and encouraged her to try one.

When Mei brought her poem to Yun, Yun was surprised to see her daughter had captured the mood she was trying to smother.

Dusk
The blood of evening glow floods westward.
The sky, dizzily purple,
blurs like a water-smudged rainbow.

Dusk
Swaying blades of grass scoop a soul chill.
The wind knifes right in the face,
attempting to cut off sad recollections.

Dusk
Whither should the noises of the heart go?
Leaden steps
hobble among the peaks of clouds.

♭ 𝄞 𝄞 𝄞 𝄞

May 16

How I wept over my marital fate in front of my daughter, a twelve-year-old. She wept with me and said I should have divorced her father. Next time she would back me up when I made a decision. If I do not have enough courage, I will never have a chance for happiness in my life. It is really an irony that my daughter should have better insight into life than me. I remembered her comments on the difference between like and love—if you like a person, you part when you begin to dislike him; if you love a person, you stay with him even when you dislike him. My tragedy is that I neither like nor love my husband. A torture for both of us.

♭ 𝄞 𝄞 𝄞 𝄞

Lately, except for cooking, Yun had to do everything in the house. Paying bills and taxes, tutoring their daughter in Chinese, having conferences with Mei's teachers, sending Long to the hospital, sending the car to the auto shop, snaking the blocked drains, pruning roses, mowing the lawn, opening and closing the window curtains, calling for roof repair, collecting rent from their two tenants. . . .*Oh, I wish somebody could share my load!* Long seemed to benefit from his inability with English. *Every single right, big or small, is yours.* When he went to the bathroom and saw the toilet was blocked by paper, he would wait for Yun to clear it up. Mei, if you truly love your father, you should teach him English. How would you two survive

if I died? But every time Long tried English, he would become
sick or have insomnia. All right, Mei, don't force him any
more. He was a delicate man, not born to wear a blue collar. But
he had to stand by the wok in a supermarket nine hours a day,
six days a week. When he came home dog-tired, face sullen
like the overcast summer sky, Yun took care not to offend him.
He was watching TV, but not English programs. Perhaps he really needed to warm up his Chinese. Being mute all year-
round, he seemed to be forgetting his mother tongue.

It was Thursday. Long had a day off. But Yun had to get up
before five to rush to the immigration office in Los Angeles to get
forms for their green cards. He did not speak English and he
had a right to sleep soundly today.

Checking her wallet, Yun only found a fifty-dollar bill. She
needed some change for parking. But instead of waking Long
up, she drove to find a store that had change. Too early—all the
stores were still closed. Finally she found an open fast-food
restaurant. The cashier said, "Sorry, we don't have twenty dollars yet. Can't you see we just opened?" Before Yun gave in to
despair, an old Mexican man waved to her. She went over, and
he took out a five-dollar bill: "Pay me back tomorrow or any
time you come by." All the other men laughed at the old fool:
"You gave her five dollars?"

Yun drove to the freeway, loving Mexicans a thousand times
more than money. She remembered how Ramon had expressed
his respect and love for his father. Unfortunately, his father was
in the hospital, having one of his legs amputated. What disease?
Diabetes. It's not a fatal disease. No, but he went to the hospital
too late. I see—he has given all his time and care to others.

The son and the father mirrored each other's nobility and
generosity. Yun was very grateful to Ramon for his willingness
to edit her manuscript. She remembered that Meng, who had
edited a translation for her in Chinese, fought about whose name
should be placed first when it was published. Prues was okay,
but he did the editing for sex and love, and he did not mind being
paid. Ramon was surprisingly different. He was willing to
help her because, as he said, the academic field today was becoming too exclusive and selfish. His pure motive magnetized
Yun even more, although she could not remove his image as a
father.

❀ ❀ ❀ ❀ ❀

May 17

I love Ramon in spite of his condescending attitude towards me. I do not need his fatherly protection, yet I love him helplessly. His noble spirit, his generosity, and his intelligence—the qualities I love best in a human being. Yet I am unable to articulate my feelings to him.

1968   Unable to say

—Meilin is in the hospital.
—What's wrong with her? She seems to be pining away.
—For Zhang Wei.
—Does he know it?
—Not until yesterday. He went to the hospital, but Meilin's mother forbade him to see her.

1975   Bitter Gourd

How many nights I murmured his name.

How many times I watched his back shadow with mute tears.

I knit a sweater and a pair of socks with wool pulled from my heart.

The moments our hands clasped and shook on the stage—he was in the role of an army commander and I, Liu Hulan, a revolutionary martyr, a marble statue at the fall of the curtain.

So many rumors about us, even though we never talked privately or exchanged a loving glance.

One day he gave me a picture of himself and asked me to show it to my parents. I kept the picture but never showed it to anybody. Love or marriage is a matter for myself. Why do I need somebody else's approval?

On the day of graduation, he said we could not be together, because I was a feelingless person, like a machine.

My eyes dried with grains of sand and I simply said goodbye.

I went back to my mother's house. The dam broke. My tears were simply oozing out mutely day and night.

My mother was chopping vegetables.

"Yun, try this crispy cucumber."

It tasted bitter.

"A woman's fate is a bitter gourd," said my mother.

❦ ❦ ❦ ❦ ❦

So passive are the plants and trees
  silently grow
          silently die
  In dire want
          they wither
                  shrivel
                      uttering no complaints
They are immovable   •
Being planted in an icy shade
  they can never march to the sunshine
    even though the heart of their leafy crown
      yearns mutely towards the heavenly stove far away

Do they know the meaning of existence
          for themselves, individually?
Their wild fruit that used to be seedy
  now becomes seedless grapes
            seedless melons
Losing their original reproductivity
  they may look even plumper and fresher
Their beauty accrues on utter self-annihilation

Plants and trees
  how impotent you are!
  You have the power to grow but
no power to kill your own excessive leaves and twigs

Do trees and flowers in a virgin forest
          need self-pruning?

You may howl with the strength of a storm
  you may clap your pulpy hands in a morning breeze
    but when you are mutilated on a sunny day
          you suffer without a groan

Who says you are the female?

❦ ❦ ❦ ❦ ❦

May 18
  Last Tuesday he suddenly appeared in my office, tall and

handsome, the image of Hercules, like sunshine enshrouding me. He came with Kan, but I knew his genuine purpose was to see me. He could not help gazing at me and then forced himself to look in a different direction. When they were leaving, I shook their hands—a significance only comprehended by him and me. (The first time when they parted he shook hands with her. The second time when he held her hands, she asked innocently, "Is handshaking an American or Chinese custom?" He smiled guilelessly, "I just want to hold your hand." He tightened his grip, she withdrew her hand and said, "Great. My hands are always cool in summer." Ever since then, handshaking has become a ritual between them—the only physical touch they could afford without a guilty conscience. Today she eagerly shook his hand.) I love to touch his hand, feeling the communicative sensitivity. Ah, communication is love. A love one cannot spell out, for fear it might fly away.

When he was gone, my officemate said to me, "You look so beautiful in this dress." I looked down at myself but saw nothing.

♦ ⚘ ⚘ ⚘ ⚘

Yun bought a large five-bedroom house, for the bank of course, as the mortgagors would say. Coming from crowded China, she felt uneasy about having three people occupying five bedrooms; on the other hand, she would have tenants to subsidize her monthly payment. As her house was located in a Chicano area, her tenants were likely to be Mexicans. Today her tenant Pedro declared he was broke, unable to pay his fifty-dollar phone bill. "Well, your phone service will be cut off then." Pedro became mad and threw all sorts of bad words at Yun, like "you racist, you Asian Scrooge, you yellow thief stealing our jobs, you think our Mexicans are liars . . . ."

Yun was absolutely stunned. She had given him a new pillow the first night because he didn't have one. Pedro said his mother in Austin needed his support so Yun exempted him from the required security deposit.

"Please move out, I cannot tolerate your racism." It was the first time Yun had used the word "racism" to a person.

During Yun's absence, Pedro had thrown his keys at her daughter and run away. A few days later, baby food coupons and magazines like *American Baby's First-Time Parents* and *First American Baby* started to come in the mail. Yun remembered Pedro's heavy-looking girlfriend. He should have told me the truth. Perhaps I could have helped them with more than fifty dollars. Yun also remembered that three days after Pedro moved in he was beaten by somebody on a bus. Perhaps he was driven out for some unpaid rent or bills. Pedro had told Yun many made-up stories, but he was not a born liar. Poverty forced him to work twelve hours a day but he ate peanut butter sandwiches all the time. He had an aged mother, he wanted a girlfriend, he loved music, he collected T-shirts, he had every right to be a man, yet it was hard to keep up a man's dignity. Yun's love for Ramon was re-making her into a more understanding human being. In China she once cruelly drove her babysitter away without buying her a train ticket.

♭ ♬ ♬ ♬ ♬

This Monday the passion between Yun and Ramon was well controlled. They talked about the great minds of the 18th Century. He did not look that handsome, his frizzy hair betrayed dots of gray, and his English had a slight Mexican Spanish flavor. Nevertheless, the rays of his mind and soul bewitched her. Her body and soul were yearning helplessly for him. She desired to read every single word he had written.

May 19
When we talked in his office professionally, we both felt elevated. Our minds darted over all sorts of subjects in a most delightful manner. When I parted from him, I immediately felt the heaviness of depression. I realize a human being is born two-faced. He may feel the same way. But one will never tell the other how one feels. Feelings are signals of truth, too fearful.

May 20
> *Our friendship—a delicious cake*
> *chilled in the refrigerator*
> *sparingly we eat*
> *Pathos lingers in the mouth*
> *Thrills of thought icily piercing*
> *so sweet*
> *so cool*
> *so cruel*

♭ ♬ ♬ ♬ ♬

It was a Friday.

He agreed to have lunch with her: "Okay, take me anywhere you want."

She came to the office early. She must have phoned his office a dozen times before noon. Perhaps he had forgotten about their appointment.

The phone rang punctually at one P.M. A few minutes later he came to meet her in the office. She stood up to go, avoiding his eyes. Yet he looked quite at ease.

"I phoned you a little earlier but you were not in. I thought you forgot about our appointment."

"I did not forget it. I was at home."

"I thought you always worked in your office on Fridays. I am sorry you made a special trip."

"Yes, I came specially to meet you. I like you."

"Oh, thank you."

Yun was wearing a long silk dress she had brought with her from China. The downward motion of the escalator, undulating, carried her like Chang E floating out from the moon. Yet, she was not conscious of her graceful movement. She felt quite shy, though she had planned it as a formal meeting, not something like a date—the idea of a "date" had never been associated with her in her whole life. She took him to the famous, expensive Chinese restaurant at the Landmark Plaza. It was the first time she had ordered Canton Dim Sum, quite a variety. But Ramon seemed to have no interest in eating.

"I never care what I eat."

"Enjoying food is enjoying life."

Last night she read through his award-winning book on John Dryden and she made some comments on the book. Being a sort of poet herself, she did not agree that poetry can be interpreted by the logic of rhetoric (perhaps she was ignorant of the true meaning of rhetoric). Nevertheless, she did enjoy reading his interpretations of Dryden's poems. The book revealed the power of his intelligence, the sensitivity of his mind, and a rare effulgence of words.

A pity, the New China Shop had gone bankrupt. It used to contain an exhibition of Chinese high art. Part of her intention was to give Ramon a guided tour through the shop.

Instead she took him to the fountain on the ground floor. They sat on the same bench. What a romantic setting. She even took out a little cassette player and put a tape inside.

"Listen to this variety of Chinese classical music. Since you're a Classicist, I think you might like it."

"Yes, it is beautiful."

"Keep it, and the player, too. And these diskettes." She took out a black box. "It took so much of your time to help me. When I am gone during the summer, you can concentrate on your own writing."

♩ ♥ ♥ ♥ ♥

May 21

Although I have been helplessly in love with him, my little present and the lunch invitation are from pure friendship and gratitude.

I showed him the poems my daughter and I wrote on Sunday. He could not read Chinese but appreciated their visible poetic form.

♩ ♥ ♥ ♥ ♥

He was very placid today, very few words. He looked at her and asked whether he could touch the material of her dress.

"Yes, of course."

"Silk?"

"Chinese silk. I've had this long dress for several years. When I was a student, I liked to wear shorter dresses."

"Shall we leave now?" She raised her watch. He held her wrist.

"Oh, I cannot see the time."

He looked at his own big watch, "Ten after three."

They walked through the underground parking lot to her car.

The car screeched and climbed up to Garvey Avenue.

"I am driving now. Why don't you talk about something?"

"I got drunk yesterday. Sorry, I cannot be lively today."

Yun remembered Prues. He drank, smoked, and got arrested for planting poppies in the woods.

"What did you drink?"

"A couple of beers."

Then he suddenly said, "If we go on like this, we will have to become lovers."

"Shall I stop?"

"It is your own choice."

She did not know why she suddenly turned bitter and sardonic.

"Of course, I love you.   But I am a disciplined woman. That's why I see you only once a week.   You are so busy and I am busy, too.   Only people of leisure can afford to play with willows and flowers."

Her outburst perhaps marked a resistance to him, since he seemed to see her as a seductive woman.   *I cannot accept any relationship if it is not based on true, sincere love.*

Back in her office, her tears showered.   She jotted a few lines in Chinese.

> *Laughing and smiling when we meet*
> *Wallowing in tears after we part*
> *Love is more painful than pain*
> *Longing is heavier than thought*
> *A passion pure and cruel like frost*
> *A self-control more severe than the jail*
> *Without clouds and rain*
> *the friendship won't last long*
> *With clouds and rain*
> *the friendship won't last long*

The last four lines in Chinese are a Catch-22.   Without getting sexually involved, a woman cannot achieve a full friendship with a man; getting involved, her friendship with him cannot last long.

♩ ♪ ♪ ♪ ♪

"Hi, Ramon.   I have some tickets for the Henan Opera, the opera of my hometown. It is completely different from Western opera.   Watching Beijing opera helped Brecht with his experimental drama.   Would you like to go?"

"When?"

"On the twenty-fourth—this coming Sunday.   I think it would be a good opportunity to expose your kids to cultural diversity.   Your wife will enjoy it, too."

After a moment of hesitation.   "Sorry, we can't.   Thank you for the offer. "

After hanging up the phone, Yun felt a bit puzzled. Am I trying to invade his territory with Chinese culture? Is he resisting my re-shaping him with my Chinese-ness?

A Chicano student came and said he wanted to study Chinese because his wife was from China. Yun eagerly offered them two opera tickets.

$ ♩ ♩ ♩ ♩

May 24

I took Mei to see the Henan Opera, the *Tragedy of Jiao Guiying.*

The story of Jiao Guiying is quite touching. She was a famous courtesan. One day she found Wang Kui dying in the snow and took him back with her. They married and pledged loyalty to each other before the Sea God. Jiao supported Wang Kui's study and later, his imperial examinations. But when Wang Kui became *Zhuangyuan*, the number one scholar in the country, he abandoned Guiying for position, fame, and a young beauty. Guiying hanged herself in the Temple of the Sea God and the Judge of the Underworld led Guiying's ghost to Wang Kui's mansion to take his life as revenge.

A very common tale, indeed. But what impressed me most is Guiying's love for Wang Kui; before she killed him, she offered to be his concubine, or maid, or the lowest servant, simply to wait on him, but Wang Kui refused her. Why does a woman in love become so subservient?

May 25

> *Early in the morning of grief and sorrow,*
> *A lost lady is longing to death for her beloved.*
> *To search for the music of the soul,*
> *   she dares to tour Hell.*
> *Let her body be torn to ten thousand shreds.*

$ ♩ ♩ ♩ ♩

Three years' stay in America could not imprint the numbers one to ten in his memory. She kept phoning Professor Martin from six to eleven, only to discover that the number Long had taken down for her was wrong. With an infinite sigh, she wrote the following:

A Dirge to Marriage

To the vast wilderness I howl hatred for him;
Autumn rain accompanies my weeping grief.
Being dumb is more a sin than being ugly;
In the belly of Zaixiang,[1] there is no space for such a boat.

I watch my tears trickling down in the twilight mirror;
A shower of bitterness hardens my heart .
How can he tolerate such an ill-yoked spouse?
The Dragon and the Clouds must get disentangled to breathe.

That evening she called Bob and also was disappointed.

> *He is already senile,*
> *In the year of a candle flickering in the wind.*
> *Gold has corroded into rotten wood.*
> *Yet, his air is still overbearing—*
> *Admirable, laughable, and irritating.*

Once Bob had asked her whether she would remember him as a distinguished scholar or as a body. She said, as a body. *Who cares about the author of those nineteen books, if I have not known you personally?* But he seemed to have misunderstood her. Over the phone, he talked about nothing but her body. An obsession with a fleshy body may destroy a person's own body.

♩ ♪ ♪ ♪ ♪

"Mei, this iron is burning hot. Don't touch it."

Yun unplugged the iron and gave her daughter a warning look.

Mei had passed her fourth birthday but still wet her pants in nursing school. The nap time during the winter is two hours long. Grown-ups hate it for being too short, while kids endure it as an endless nightmare. Imprisoned in a small crib, a child dares not turn her body, let alone go to the bathroom. This repressive experience would perhaps make Mei a wakeful person all her life. You could scare her by simply ordering her to take a

---

[1] Zaixiang, prime minister of imperial China, is known for his broadmindedness.

nap. She was lucky to have come to America to escape naps.

"Why, Mom?" Mei was inquisitive. Children were far too inquisitive.

"Why? Electricity has made the iron hot."

"But it's not red like fire." Mei was not convinced.

That evening Mei refused to let her mom wash her right hand.

"Dear me! It's burnt." Yun grabbed that little claw from her back.

Now Mei was nearly thirteen. She loved mathematics, algebra, or any subject in science. Yun, though once a first place winner in a junior high math contest, had long said goodbye to science. Her emotions and sentiments grew with her age. Twenty years ago, while seeing *A White-Haired Girl*, her teacher's tears dropped like rain on Yun's shoulder but her nose merely twitched to drive away some sourness. Then she squared her shoulders. Now a shred of favor, kindness, or generosity would stir Yun's heart like a gentle finger touching the leaves of Shy-grass. There was no more rationality, no more logic. Disbelief of science stole into her intuitive body.

Yun's teeth are like her northerner father's, big and uneven. Flanking the front are two sharp ones that the Chinese call "tiger fangs." Everybody in the family knows she has the most unsightly but useful teeth. Long cannot eat anything tough like a steak and Mei does not like crispy apples. But Yun can chew almost everything. One evening when she called home saying she was terribly hungry but did not have time to come home, Mei joked: "Mom, why don't you bite your desk?"

"I could, if it were not made of plastic and iron."

Mei and Yun went shopping on Saturday. A new product caught their eye.

"Look, Mom, you must buy this Natural White. It will whiten your tiger fangs and make you look young." Yun knew her daughter wanted to use her as an experiment again. Nevertheless, she was persuaded.

Yun tried it for a couple of days. A hoax! There was no pleasant bubbling sound during the process of oxygenation. Everything was deceptive nowadays. "No, Mom. I don't think so. Do the directions say that some teeth will take sixty times? Yours are definitely the toughest teeth in America."

The directions say one should only use a thin layer. Yun had no patience. The layer she applied to her teeth was so thick one night that a tiny bit slipped to her lower lip. She heard a sizzling sound as if an engineer from the Land of Ants was drilling her lip. The sound was pleasant and thrilling, because it was really burning in the flesh. Bones had no feelings.

♩ ♫ ♫ ♫ ♫

May 26

Ramon gave me a copy of his book, under an elegant red cover, with a long handwritten letter. The words in the letter plucked the strings of my heart with their noble fingers. Since I had read the manuscript carefully, the contents of the book already were old friends, as its images and power of diction had been absorbed into me. However, the letter further convinced me of the distance between us. He might be too noble, too paternalistic for me. His analogy of his love for children, his statement of enjoying "giving" rather than "receiving," forms a hierarchy between us. No, I did not give anything to him as a "gift"—the music and the disks are shared with him. As I said, they are nothing but an extension of me.

> *He is the Rocky Mountains*
> *snow-capped with nobility*
> *a forbidden height*
> *an icy-cruel purity*
> *I wish I could be a snow-lotus*
> *to match his beauty*
> *Yet I am merely a blade of grass*
> *in a corner ostracized by the Land of Angels*
> *turning green and yellow*
> *at the mercy of Heaven*
> *I must trespass*
> *to tap water from stones.*

May 27

Random thoughts on reading tales about women and poems by women throughout Chinese history:

A female is nothing but a body to the opposite sex. As she is said to have no soul, the body is all. The one whose body is sullied must commit suicide.

The body of a woman is all and nothing. To prove her

determination, she shaves off her ears and blinds her eyes. Then people can hear through her body. Self-mutilation is a form of speech.

In order to make herself seen and heard, Wang Zhaojun had to deport her body to the barbarians.

Li Qingzhao's bodily image as a pining yellow flower has surpassed all her poetry.

Cai Wenji was captured by the barbarians and her body was not only sullied but fractured by separation of mother from children. At the complete loss of her body, her lamenting voice came to be heard down through history. Quite an exception? No. Cai Wenji to men is not a female, but a scapegoat of a nation under foreign invasion.

Plato wrote about the ladder of beauty—from love of the body to love of the soul to love of absolute beauty.

Romanticists hold the body above the mind. After all, the body generates powerful emotions and passion.

Postmodernists separate the body from the soul, love from sex, and sex from the body. One can give sex as a friendly gift, a gesture of sympathy, a release of tension. What's sex to do with the body, if the act does not bring sexual diseases to the body? If a person can take sex so lightly, he or she will not suffer too much from psychological problems.

Partnership—cooperation.

No marital bondage but family.

Love/spirit/soul are forever individualistic. They belong to the loner—*I wander alone like a cloud.*

Love no longer needs the fleshy body!

Body/sex are no longer a treat to me.

If we cannot reach a more intimate communication without breaking the tension between sexes, let us share our bodies and then discard them.

Throughout history, a female, like duckweed floating in a pond, searches for a master or a home to anchor herself.

The impossibility of marriage does not imply the impossibility of sexual and spiritual love—only that there is less chance to possess or be possessed.

Does the desire to love stem from the desire to possess or be possessed? No, it is a desire to be with, to share the time.

I only want to share the emotion and soul of a being I love. Emotion and soul increase in the process of sharing.

May 28

Every Thursday morning when I think of him so intensely, my tears roll out like beads off two strings. The dog outside the window fiercely scratches the window glass.

I have an unquenchable desire to commune with his soul, a desire stronger than death.

The intensity is like the suffocated, overcast summer sky. Only the release of water can cleanse it. When autosexuality fails, the intensity wrings water from every cell of my body —nothing but a stubborn loving soul anchored in the sea of the body.

The Thinking of Him

The thinking makes me dizzy
The thinking produces unconscious smiles
The thinking siphons tears
The thinking pushes me to the drowning sea
The thinking leads me to the Land of Death
The thinking paints infinite mirages
*   but a single hope.*

May 29

Ramon and I had lunch at a Sichuan restaurant. Today he dressed very smartly—brown pants, light gray shirt—looking elegant and tall. I remembered his comments about how I looked last time. He seemed to be worried about my reaction to him being a Mexican-American. Of course I knew his roots the moment he talked about Mexican culture and people with such passion. Before I moved to Los Angeles I never had any contact with Mexicans. Through people like Carlos and Ramon, I came to see that the Mexicans share many traditional values with the Chinese: loyalty to parents, love of children, hard work, generosity to others.

Who is Carlos? Yun's former tenant, a trucker, a soccer player. He said Yun's sitting room had no life and showed her his own room. Well, it was full of life indeed. About a dozen soccer trophies demonstrated his glorious past. Among his huge posters Yun recognized Marilyn Monroe and Elvis Presley. As his room was extra-king sized, he even had his weight-lifting equipment right at his bedside. On the wall behind the TV Yun saw a photo of a woman in a bikini. She recognized her as the lady who visited him once a week. The lady's blond hair looked too artificial, the powder on her face seemed to be falling off all the time, and her over-mascaraed eyes made her look like a witch. She came usually on Carlos's payday and often left in an hour.

Carlos was not a bad storyteller. When he first moved in he told Yun he was not married. He did not want to buy a house because he was planning to marry a woman who owned a house. "You know, a man like me is very useful around the house. I can do all sorts of things, lawn, sink, garden. Whenever you need help, let me know." Before long Carlos forgot his story and showed Yun a picture of his four boys and said his ex-wife and the kids were in San Francisco. He was paying $800 a month to support them.

"Why did you come to Los Angeles? Being a trucker, you can find a job in San Francisco."

"Well, a man cannot be tied down by family and kids. I need my individualism."

Carlos did have his individualism. He would not work on Saturdays and Sundays. "Five working days are enough to support a man." Every weekend he would put on a tie and an expensive suit. After he left for a decent restaurant or church, his strong cologne lingered in the house. Compared with Carlos, Yun felt her own existence was pitiful: reading, writing, teaching, house work. . . no fun at all.

Once or twice Carlos dragged Yun and her daughter to a swap meet. There he would greet all sorts of Mexican men like old brothers. Carlos neither drank nor smoked. One could hardly find any vices in him. He helped Yun change the oil in her car and fix faucets. Each time he would expect Yun to pay for his value of labor. Once, when Mei sprained her toe while exercising, he dipped her toe into hot water and massaged it like a Chinese doctor. Mei's pain was gone the following day. Another time, hot cooking oil left a big blister on Yun's arm. When Carlos saw it, he immediately used an onion to suck the liquid from the blister, saying that if one did not get the liquid out, it would not only take an awful long time to heal but would leave a black print on the skin. It was true. Yun could still see the dark area left by a burn on one of her hands. This time, the blister left quickly and did not leave a scar. Carlos was full of practical wisdom, and he would not take anything for these services.

One day he and Yun drove to Pepboy to buy a part for her car. Carlos said, "You smell fishy."

"Sorry, I was too busy to take a shower this morning."

"No, I mean the smell your husband left on you last night."

Yun knew what he was driving at and said frankly, "Sorry, I do not like that kind of joke. I am Chinese and I am not used to it."

"All right, but what's wrong with sex? It makes a person sleep well and relaxed. We often talk sex at work."

"Not with me. I have to tell you that we must stay away from sex if we want to be friends."

"Right, I agree with you. Sex often destroys the friendship between a man and a woman. How old are you? Over forty? I can't believe it. Many Mexican women are overused by men. They age far too early."

Many times when Yun referred to her husband she used "she." It was perhaps an innocent habit because "he" and "she" and "it" were all pronounced the same way in Chinese. But Carlos did not let this pass.

"Ha, ha, you always treat your husband like a wife. You married a weak husband because you are afraid of strong men. Look at my rolling muscles."

♭ ♯ ♯ ♯ ♯

Like her, Ramon was quite restrained in his emotion towards the other.

He had a highly selective memory—automatically forgetting trivial things. He no longer remembered which way they took to Monterey Park last Friday. Yun said, I hope you won't forget *me* too soon.

After lunch, they each chose a fortune cookie. His advised him to continue giving and gain knowledge in the process of giving and hers told her to continue expanding her horizons. Such coincidence made her almost superstitious.

After lunch, he went to her office to edit her proposal for the annual meeting of the Modern Languages Association.

♭ ♯ ♯ ♯ ♯

May 29

How I treasured the moment we sat close together before the screen. Our hands and arms touched innocently from time to time like a breeze kissing wild grass, producing thrills of physical sensitivity—such sublimity, perhaps, exists only between lovers. Not only our minds but our bodies yearn for each other. When I think of him, my throat becomes so dry that I feel like an exhausted camel gasping in the desert.

✿ ✿ ✿ ✿ ✿

She thought of the passion she captured the moment she was inspired by her idol of Romanticism. Now Ramon, a real man of masculine beauty, had aroused not only her passion but sensitivity and sensuality. Perhaps because his image loomed too large over her, she was awed.

✿ ✿ ✿ ✿ ✿

May 30
"Please, no more gifts. I appreciate your gratitude—especially since this world is generally an ungracious one. Friendship is enough. For me, giving is more important than receiving. As I tell my children, they owe me nothing, but if they ever have children, they will repay me by giving to them what they have received from me. I would expect you too, if you wish, to repay me by helping someone in the future in the same way. I have been disappointed, though not surprised, by the scarcity of generosity among academics. Perhaps that is the way of the world, but I will never subscribe to it. I have been a soldier, a coast guard, and now a teacher, and I have learned to stand alone and survive. Those few people in my life who have helped me, I can never repay, except in the small way I am assisting you, for example. . . ."

I have read Ramon's letter at least three times and each time I feel more deeply touched than before. I got a spanking for my failure to recite a four-line Tang poem at the age of five; yet, how easily I memorized every word of his letter.

✿ ✿ ✿ ✿ ✿

She did not stop at reciting. She borrowed books on Mexican history and culture. She was overjoyed to find out in a recently published Chinese encyclopedia that Chinese Buddhist monks

visited Mexico as early as 458 A.D. And the unearthed tablet in-
scriptions in Mexico revealed striking similarities to the
Chinese in figures and pictorial characters. Their customs,
legislation, and calendar also had parallels with the Chinese.

♩ ♪ ♪ ♪ ♪

Guadalupe had been living in Yun's house free for ten days.
She moved in saying that she had a regular job at a Glendora
hospital, but she did not. Every day she stayed in her small
room, staring at the walls. The second month she said her wallet had been stolen by a thief and she lost the five hundred dollars she had withdrawn from the bank for her rent and food. By
and by she confessed that she did not have a penny in the bank.

"Why don't you apply for Social Security as many others
did?"

" Well, I still want to work. I am not that old yet."

"But how can you find a job by staying at home all day
long?"

"I've tried, but I don't have a chance."

She was right. Even Carlos had been without a job for three
months now. He had moved to a cheaper place, though he often
dreamt of having his large room back.

"Why don't you go to your son?"

"My son is in prison."

"In prison? For what?"

"He killed his wife. It happened three years ago. It was reported in the *Tribune*. Everybody in this neighborhood knew,
I'm sure. That year I sold my house and gave my son 50,000 dollars so that he could make a down-payment on a house so that his
kids would have a nice home to live in and I could move in and
take care of them. My God, when my son got the money he
bought himself a motorcycle and squandered the rest like water.
He had many women running after him. . . ."

"How old was he then?"

" Twenty-two."

" Too immature to have that much money, I guess."

" You're right. He murdered his wife one night. Even though
I am his mother, I think a thirteen-year sentence is too lenient
for such a wicked crime."

"Have you ever thought that your son was killed by the
money you gave him when he was not ready to use it properly?"

"Right, I feel guilty. But I am a human being. I have been

good to my husband and he divorced me for my kindness. And I ruined my son for loving him too much. Now I have no friends, no relatives to turn in this world."

"Where's your boyfriend?"

"Oh, that evil man. He took my car and never turned back."

"I know he will never come back here again because he is afraid of paying rent and the fifty dollars he borrowed from me. But once you leave here you will see him."

"Really?"

"Believe me. You and he are natives. Ho does not even speak English well but you are educated. You can run his business."

"Can I?"

"Of course, you can."

Guadalupe left the following day with a confident smile.

A seed knows how to sprout once it tumbles out of a glass bottle.

Am I trying to pay Ramon back in the small way I can?

✿ ❦ ❦ ❦ ❦

June 1

Friday, Simon called me for lunch. I declined because of my previous appointment with Ramon. Simon seems to be in agony these days. Though I received him as a friend because of our chat, I could not bear seeing his image—pitiful and aggressive simultaneously. I still remember the day he burst out complaining on the phone, making me feel extremely awkward in front of my officemate. Out of compassion I made a special trip to school to talk with him.

He is, after all, a shockingly frank person, admirably. In our contact, he has never tried to deceive me; instead, he informed me of his disadvantages: his deaf father, his poor health condition, his intimate relationships with two girls, his unsuccessful academic career. . . . In a way, his frankness estranged me.

Nevertheless, he seemed to fall in love with me. And he thought I felt the same way. He blamed me for treating him like a stranger when we met in the corridor; he encouraged me not to behave like a rabbit when coming into contact with a man; he told me that a faculty member's sexual behavior should be separate from professional promotions. . . .

I said, "I am a married woman and I do care about my reputation."

He looked disappointed, not expecting me to be so conservative.

But my cautiousness had been purchased at a high price in China.

Honestly, even in China, I was not a conservative woman and rebellion is in my nature.

I told him that I do not break codes unless I feel a need to—for instance, if I fall in love with someone.

Then he said he wants to have a friend, not someone he sees once a week or once a month. And he was thinking of inviting me to a party, but restrained himself for fear of my declining.

I see I should liberate him from this illusion.

"Ever since we chatted and confided in each other about our personal problems, I indeed have taken you to be a friend. During the LA riots, I was worried about you. If I had your home number, I would have called you. However, I have to tell you that I am not in love with you and I do not wish to lead you in that direction and I am not going to marry you. We can be friends but never sexual friends."

I even told him the reasons: You have led a bohemian life while I have been a conservative wife—our lifestyles do not fit together. (He chuckled. And I could not laugh because I was too serious in telling him the lie. Who cares about his lifestyle, if I truly love him?) And your health is scary. Did you say that you could not marry the first girl because of your health?

Out of ignorance, I tend to associate any unfamiliar health condition with the terrible AIDS virus. It was shockingly frank of me to declare that I would not enter into a sexual relationship with anyone in America unless I was sure of the person's condition.

Simon laughed and said I was damned practical. "Do you mean you demand a man to show a doctor's proof before going to bed?"

"Not necessarily. What is important is my own trust."

Such a horrible denunciation and suspicion. Perhaps I have been too frank; yet my frankness is a reaction to his.

I feel sorry for the love I cannot afford as a gesture of compassion. I do not hate any man who falls in love with me, because being loved is a nice feeling and loving another being is a human right. I will never repeat the first error I committed in my relationship with a man—turning a lover into an alien.

June 2

Every morning I listen to the Chinese song "Why is the flower so red?" when my thoughts about Ramon become intolerably painful. He seems to have been callous to a sensitive soul. I have asked twice about the novel he wrote, because I wished to read his words to dispel the unspeakable pain.

I am afraid that I have fallen in love again with an image created by myself. Perhaps I need to know more about the reality.

Only the cruel reality can shatter my dream.

Impossibility can restrict but can never kill the love.

Only disillusionment can act as the murderer.

I fear it's coming—the moment I will become disillusioned about him and he about me.

No. I refuse to accept such disillusionment.

For our friendship, I would sacrifice all pleasures, ready to wade through the sea of pain.

♩ ❦ ❦ ❦ ❦

For a moment she divided her role between lover and cool psychiatrist. She discovered how one's words can betray and conceal a lover.

—Can I buy something for your son's graduation? (A desire to be his son's godmother, or a token of my gratitude for his help to me?)

—Can I give two tickets to you and your wife for a vacation in Hawaii? (How I wished I could travel alone with him to paradise.)

—Your wife's name, Ylia, is beautiful. She has part-time job? A teaching aide in a primary school? That's what I would like to do—only work a couple of hours a day. (A subconscious desire to replace her.)

In a sense, a lover never tells a lie. Yet, every word is a camouflage, a signal. It throws the speaker off guard.

Words are such clever devices for revising, substituting, disguising thoughts. This psychological phenomenon gave her an urge to read Freud and Jung again.

♩ ❦ ❦ ❦ ❦

June 3

Wednesday evening after six o'clock was our time to meet for a chat. I had been longing for that moment. But when it finally came, he was not there—a seemingly deliberate absence, a conspiracy to kill me. The other day I joked about his obliviousness to me, that he should have forgotten me so soon. A swoon came over me—if I had fainted, I would have suffered less pain. I must be experiencing death—who says death knows no pain? I never expected God to punish me so cruelly.

> *A soul was screaming like a wounded beast*
> *but without its freedom to release agony to the wilderness*
> *A suppressed moan*
> *from a sinner pressed at the bottom of Hell.*

I muffled my sobs, for fear of ears beyond the walls of my office.

What is more painful than a person in love?

I saw Simon, that poor man, sandy hair flying in all directions, wandering like a lost soul in the corridor—so much so, a parody of myself.

> *What turmoil of emotions I had experienced*
> *weeping*
>   *moaning*
>   *humming the saddest tune*
>   *singing most cheerful songs*
>   *trying to grade papers*
> *All the desperation to collect a splitting soul.*
> *Is there a substitute?*
> *Is there a transference?*

> *Sappho, where is the Leucadian cliff?*

> *I wish I had a bottle of alcohol or a dose of cocaine*
> *I am too sober*
>   *the pain is too keen.*
> *I wish I could dissipate myself in the house of whores. . .*
> *I know I have been love-sick*
> *I have been trying to be my own doctor*
> *I am confident of my power to cure myself*
> *I see myself sinking to the waist in a swamp*
> *I know if I do not stop I will die*

Am I too much of a traditional woman?
Why should I have been torturing myself so?
Why should I have been repressing myself like this?
Why should I live in prison or a cocoon woven by myself?

I must stop this pathological development.

I must talk with him and I wish to hear him declare the words I declared to that sandy-haired man: I do not love you and I am not going to marry you. I like you, but merely as an intellectual being.

Even if he says he loves me, let me hear that his wife and children are far more precious and sacred to him.

I wish to hear his denial of all possibilities between us. Condemn me, condemn me to eternal abandonment and loneliness.

A long awaited moment
a cruel absence
perhaps a deliberation
murdered a love-sickened soul by shredding its nerves
A baby's cry smothered with a pillow
Choked tears tumbling down without a sound
for fear of strange ears beyond the walls
outside the corridor.

Prescription from Dr. Hu:

1. Tell him straightforwardly how I feel.

2. Let him tell all the impossibles, or better—no love at all.

3. A potion for disillusionment to prevent another stroke of heavenly pain.

Waking up past twelve, I wept again. Three tearful showers are not enough to cleanse my soul. Oh, how I wish I could die.

Did he say he has two grown children and an intelligent wife?

The satisfied never know the suffering of the starved. What a chasm between us. Perhaps he has been living happily in a banal way. Even if his heart were disturbed, he would not have the courage to break the moral bond to his family. On the other hand, the torture of my marriage has honed me too eagerly for a fall into a love-trap.

The heart is a lonely hunter; yet, instead of hunting anything, it is more often hunted or haunted.

♩ ❦ ❦ ❦ ❦

The following day, Ramon smiled apologetically. He said
his car had broken down on the way. His son was with him and
he could not call her. Yun could well imagine that he drove the
shabbiest car among the professors. He was not ashamed of
being poor. Perhaps only a rough life can forge a tough being,
balanced between brain and brawn. Yun remembered Ramon
saying that he had reroofed his own house. She immediately vi-
sualized a bear-like shadow who, carrying piles of tiles, climbs
up and kneels on a burning roof under the hot sun or on an icy
roof in dark winter, putting down one tile after another deftly
like a Chinese lady working on her embroidery.

♩ ❦ ❦ ❦ ❦

The phone finally rang.
— Hi, Ramon. I had a dream last night. I hope you can help
me figure out what it means.

*The concrete wall is hard, straight, and high. I am
climbing it with great effort. It is too hard because I am
holding a ring of keys in one of my hands. The man
on the top of the wall waves to me. The moment I give
him the keys, the wall becomes soft and yielding. It
bends to me like a springy tree trunk so that I climb
with my feet easily holding to the nicks between the
bricks.*

— Well, it sounds very architectural. Do you wear any
clothes in the dream?
— I do not know. But I am certainly not wearing high heels.

♩ ❦ ❦ ❦ ❦

June 5
Again Friday. We met for lunch. His clothes had a sort of
crude drabness, and he looked gravely serious. If I had not
known about his intelligence and generous heart, it would have
been hard for me to be attracted to this type of person. But love
has blinded me to all appearances. I longed for communica-

tion. However, we did not talk much during the meal. He finished his even before I started. I became aware of being watched and realized it must be painful for him to watch me—a waste of time he never had to bear in his life.

"I am going to the library on my way back."

"Why don't you go now?"

He smiled but stayed.

We talked about the pleasure of reading in a place like Walden Pond. He has been to New England and seen the pond.

"Actually I can read anywhere, and wherever I can read is my Walden Pond."

A man does everything according to his will and the circumstances seem to create no agitation.

"Do you want to go to Hawaii?"

"No."

"I'm going, of course, not with you but with my daughter. "

How I wish I could go with him to some unknown place to share a moment of solitude.

" Would you like to have lunch at my house someday?"

A slip of the tongue or an unconscious seduction?

"I do not go to any faculty members' homes."

I realized how improper my suggestion was, particularly between opposite sexes. Did I ever dream of having him in my room or in a hotel or somewhere?

A slip of the tongue is perhaps a glimpse of the subconscious. I could not articulate it if I were conscious.

"Are you disturbed by me?"

"No."

"I can stop."

Silence. A silence distorted by pain. The atmosphere between us was oppressive. I am not used to oppression; I am a liberated being, or struggling to be one.

It gradually dawned on me that we had become more and more obscure to one another through our mutual attraction and suppression. The ice must be broken if we want to breathe. Sometimes, bodily contact can remove obstacles and lead to intimate communication. Bodily contact can work as an emancipative factor. However, there must be some other means to break the barrier when one cannot afford the price of the body.

✦ ✿ ✿ ✿ ✿

That evening Yun stammered out the truth.

She told him how she had fallen in love with him lately, how she had cried, and how abnormally she had behaved when he failed to keep the appointment.

She said she told him all this because she believed only he, he alone, could set her free from the intolerable pain and psychological chaos she was experiencing.

—You like me, have an interest in me as an intelligent woman; but I love you. There's a distance between like and love. Logically, I am suffering more psychologically than you are. You are a Classicist (used to being self-contained); but I am a Romanticist, whose emotions build up quickly to an insufferable intensity. . . .

—Let me say something as a doctor. A person obsessed by love has the desire to possess. . . .

—No. I have no such desire. I've passed through three stages of love in my life. First, I could not separate love from marriage. At the failure of love, I married a man I did not love as transference. When I was in love the second time, I mixed love with the body. (She did not tell him that to save herself she resorted to profaning the body.) Now I've reached a new stage. What I long for is communication.

Now she realized that she had been tortured miserably, partly because of a lover's longing to be convinced of love from the loved.

—You do not love me, do you?

Silence. Too much responsibility to admit, if it were true; too much responsibility if it were not true. A prolonged silence.

—Do you want to go to bed with me?

He was so frank. She batted her wide-open eyes like a child.

—No. Although eroticism intensifies my emotions and I do not believe in chastity, I fear the involvement of family, children, and the scandal. . . .

She could not believe what she had just said to him—those stereotyped worries that she had never thought about during her moments of longing.

—You are wise. Then let us keep our professional relationship. You can take me as your brother, if you wish.

—Perhaps I have been too aggressive, acting like a Spenserian seductress or enchantress.

—I am not a victim.

He must feel insulted. No one can make the other a victim without his or her complicity.

✿ ✿ ✿ ✿ ✿

June 6

Reviewing my life, I want to laugh. It is unlucky for me, a woman of forty, to still have the passion of an eighteen-year-old. Though I have been loved by quite a few men, each time I fell in love, I was doomed to suffer the agony of the unrequited. Nothing could match the intensity of my passion dragged through the trial of death. It has always taken a long time for me to recover, even by means of transference. Fortunately, my intellectual faculty has been sharpened rather than damaged during each emotional upheaval.

As I became myself again through my talk to Ramon, I feel my gratitude for him growing. It is for my sake he never articulates his own feelings. What a strong will he needs to protect me.

Before I made my confession, he told me about his two years' experience in war. He shot enemies. He was shot at, showers of bullets. When he was a coast guard, he shot a criminal right in the chest in self-defense. The war experience alienated him from the world for quite some time.

"I went to war voluntarily while the Caucasians generally don't. We love America and believe in patriotism. . . ."

"You mean pacifism?"

"Yes, my war experience did lead me to pacificism. I took to literature, partly to nurse my soul."

Once he was a high IQ kid at school, preparing to be a great physicist. After the war, he turned to literature to nurture the wounds in his soul. He has indeed turned into a man of gentle love and sensitivity, though the potential for violence is still inside him.

"Yes. The violence in me will break out whenever I need to defend myself."

He is a heroic as well as a dangerous man.

At one point, perhaps as a slip of the tongue, he mentioned cocaine. He immediately said it was a joke. He never took drugs. But I believe he knows the taste of drugs.

Now the shore has been cleared. Not only his family ties make our coming together impractical, but his lonely habits, drinking, and potential for violence also forbid further development of our intimacy.

Is analysis the process of disillusionment?

Yet, love is a fallacy. I do not feel my love for him is lessened by his stories or my analysis.

♦ ❦ ❦ ❦ ❦

Every time she sees Simon, her sympathy deepens. The pain she has suffered lately enables her to understand the emotional convulsion another person has been going through. He invited her for lunch again and she declined. This Friday his gruff voice betrays a pretended coldness. *Perhaps he has seen Ramon and me together. Perhaps he is trying to regain his emotional balance as I have done.* Nevertheless, humans are such pitiful beings in the world. Love is privileged play for them, yet the price is too high. Trees and flowers do not have the choice of love. The wind blows the pollen to mate and produce seeds. Animals, particularly domestic ones, do not have the freedom of emotional love but a biological need. Their masters simply take them out to mate for the type of offspring they want.

♦ ❦ ❦ ❦ ❦

June 7

That evening when I was leaving, Ramon was fumbling with his files. I was not sensitive enough to appreciate it as a transferred action to harness himself.

After all, it seems too childish for adults to play the game of pain. Now I come to see why he laughed when I said in an outburst, "Of course, I love you."

He is no superman; he must be caught in the game, too.

♦ ❦ ❦ ❦ ❦

Ramon and Yun met in his office. He had tried to hide from her for the past two weeks while she was achieving a gradual recovery.

Her mood was particularly good today. He looked calm, and gave her a paternal smile. From a few words, such as "my family is the chain around my neck" (he made a strangling gesture) and "responsible" and "self-control," she gathered that in the past two weeks he had gone through a severe trial. His desire is strong, but his will is stronger. Though he suffered he came out a winner or a victim of morality.

No doubt, he is patriarchal or, at least, condescending towards me. Yet I am irresistibly attracted to him, perhaps by his power of self-control or his inscrutability. How I desire to read his novel—a hundred fragments, he said. Yet, he deliberately hides it from me. He says he is afraid that if I read it I would be disappointed. But he also says he will not write anything ordinary. His is an experiment in form. Writing a novel is prostituting oneself in the Emperor's new clothing. Perhaps his novel is too private, as is the one I am writing at the moment.

The reader could threaten or manipulate the writer once the reader reads the writer's soul inside out. The novel can be published because the public is insensitive. Even if the public were sensitive, being so distant from the writer, they do not constitute a threat or power that can manipulate the writer. Therefore, even between close friends, it is unwise to be too intimate. "Fences keep good neighbors"—a line from Frost's wise poem blared from the recording Mei was playing.

That night, after he told his stories about the Vietnam War, Yun recited Li Bo's famous drinking poem and explained how the drunken poet, the moon, and the shadow form a delightful "unclinging relationship." Their lofty, ennobling tie depends on the moon, who is unable to comprehend the cause of the poet's drinking; it wanders to and fro with the poet. And the shadow, though following him all the time, never enters him. Thus, the poet is forever a loner—only such a loner can fully enjoy the freedom of his soul. When the poet is awake, the tripartite share pleasure; when the poet gets lost in his drunkenness, the tripartite disperse. Yet based on unclingingness, their friendship is immortal. The lover does not suffer the pain of longing or anxiety of waiting. The human relationship should, perhaps, be modeled after things in nature. It seemed that her subconscious desire for such a relationship led her to reciting that poem before her confession of love.

The moment she was making her confession, another self stood watching her stutter like a nervous patient. This self knew clearly that she was resorting to the last straw—a talking cure. And the process of this articulation is the process of killing the angel of love in a lover. This self was aware that her words were contradictory and confusing.

She felt guilty. But she was not aware of how tyrannical, manipulative, and selfish she had been in the whole process. Her confession had been intended to disentangle herself from the bog of love. As an intelligent man, he chose to do exactly what she wanted.

Even though she was wicked and selfish, she tasted the pain

of true love.

True love turns every woman into Lin Daiyu, who is destined to repay with tears the man who has nurtured her love—the liquidation of the body. In spite of a full awareness of the trap, Yun wept hopelessly day and night. When her tears stopped, the music wrung from the strings of *Er Hu* continued her lamentation.

After her confession, Yun gradually shortened her tearful indulgence to about an hour in the morning.

Articulation helped her gain a new equilibrium.

Monday she phoned him. He asked her how she was. She said, "After talking I found myself better, cured." She did not see him the whole week, as he was busy with students' final examinations. The following week, the last week of the quarter, she gave him the last part of her manuscript, the afterword, to edit. When she finally saw him the following Monday, he had not finished editing it, but mentioned that he was going to disappear. She joked, disappear from the earth? He replied, perhaps. She immediately sensed a sign of farewell. *Are you traveling anywhere? No, just staying at home. Then, you are only escaping one person—me. Silence.* Now she realized how wicked and inconsiderate her confession had been. From his very few words about self-control, she became conscious of how he had been tortured and distracted in the past two weeks.

He had fallen in love with her, perhaps even more strongly than she with him. She apparently wronged him by stating that he only liked her as an intellectual being but she loved him; therefore, she suffered more than he.

"I wanted my candid talk with you the other day to remove the bodily obstacles between our communication. It seems just the opposite happened. I regret that my confession has alienated us. I did not expect to be so wicked."

"No, it is not your fault. It is a matter of personal control. I won't allow myself to do any harm to you and my body does not belong to myself."

"What do you mean, your body does not belong to yourself? What kind of harm can you possibly do to me? Like you, I am a moralist and a responsible being. I restrain myself for the sake of your family and your children."

Then she told him quite humorously that in her life she had fallen in love only three times and each was unrequited.

He protested the term "unrequited" and said—if I were single, if I had space of my own . . . . It can be true that a married man does not have a room of his own, just as Victorian women had been denied this space.

Although she was married, she had always kept her own room and had space of her own. This space, if not for the same purpose as that claimed by other feminists, was a space for her sentimental indulgence. She had the freedom to shed tears upon her pillow and jot down her pain on paper or to transfer her love to reading at any time of the day or night. More than laughing, now she found herself enjoying weeping, a purging release. As long as a woman is able to weep, she will never be neurotic. Weeping silently is a woman's catharsis.

Yes, a man in love must suffer more than a woman, if he is too strong-willed to loosen himself in a pool of tears.

That was a most unforgettable night. Their hearts started to mingle through the interflow of words. The angel of love in both had been killed. One was no longer clinging to the other.

"Bye-bye. Perhaps I'll see you next quarter, since you do not wish to see me anymore."

"Who says I do not wish to see you?"

"You said you are going to disappear."

"Oh, only for two weeks. Afterwards I will always be in my office. You are the person who is going away. Aren't you going to Hawaii?"

"Yes. I am going with my daughter. We both plan to write a sort of personal novel—an utter abandonment of the self to suit the nature there."

♩ ♫ ♫ ♫ ♫

In her dream, Yun heard a mermaid singing:

> *I am the romantic sea*
> *surging with passions*
> *You are the classical coast*
> *chaining me with dead sand*
> *No matter how I lap at your lips*
> *no matter how I scream billows of love*
> *the coast is mute and calm*
> *pinchering the sea with its silent principle*
> *Before the beginning of the world*
> *the universe was filled with wanton water*

When sand gave shape to the sea
there rose the virtues of humanity
Once the sea was so powerful
it broke the chain of coast
and deluged the whole world
When the coast asserts itself again
it guards the sea so vigilantly
No hope of another deluge
There is no coast without sea
No sea without coast.

Yun was enchanted by the singing. In the twilight zone she struggled to watch herself in a different dream.

She is thinking of stopping. That voice urges her, "Crawl on, there's light at the end of the tunnel." She gropes steadily ahead. She is going to stop again. That voice calls, "Look, look at that chink." She struggles on desperately. When she staggers to the place where the light has been blinking at her, she sees another dark tunnel leading as if to Nowhere. A sign is posted there: "Tunnel at the end of the light!" Her toes are all swollen, her fingernails, discolored, start bleeding. She stops. Lifting her head, she sees a sky of light above. She grins wryly, "Why are my eyes always looking ahead, not above?"

Looking above is easy, but it has to be purchased in tunnels of pain.

June 26

It was the last Friday of June.

What a blissful night. He escorted me to the parking structure in his old role of a coast guard. I extended my hand to him for a final goodbye.

"Let me give you a hug."

I did not know how our bodies touched—a moment too sacred even for memory—but I remember how suddenly he tore himself away from me and strode into the darkness. How much can a man control himself? Just look at him.

Even since I fell in love with him, the scene of Tristan and

Isolde, of two naked bodies lying divided by a sword in an icy cave has repeatedly appeared before my eyes. As long as we keep the sword in sight, our bodies will be pure. What is the sword? My tyranny? His nobility? Our morality, cowardice, limits of horizon? I do not know. But the sword is shimmering coldly there. Although the angel of sexual love has been denied in me, another kind of love is forever reserved for him in my heart. I seem to have heard the shared music from our souls for one moment. Then it disappeared. What's left remains a memory, clinging and unclinging to me.

Coda

The search for music of the soul is what gives meaning to a person's existence. Bo Ya was the best musician of the Spring and Autumn Period (221-722 B.C.). What he played on the string instrument was lofty and profound, above common understanding. Only one person, Zhong Ziqi, could comprehend his musical message. When Bo Ya played one tune, Zhong Ziqi said: "Majestic like the lofty mountain"; when Bo Ya played another tune, he said: "Undulating like a flowing river." Zhong Ziqi captured perfectly the soul of Bo Ya's music. Later, Zhong Ziqi died. Losing his only communicative listener, Bo Ya smashed his instrument and abandoned playing. Thus the Chinese descendants understand the importance of a unique friend in one's life who is able to appreciate the music of the soul. Bo Ya is a musician of high art. Even a musician of lower art finds the meaning of his playing or artistic existence through the communication between his composition and his listener. Thus the Chinese believe the greatest frustration in one's life is playing a fine tune in front of a cow. It is not because the cow is dumb, but because the audience is inappropriate.

He happened to be born in the year of the cow and he has been so indifferent to my passions. It is such an irony that I should keep playing my tune, composing music with tears and pain from my soul in front of a Classicist who strangles our spontaneous flow of feelings mercilessly.

The lofty art of Bo Ya was not easily gained. Although he learned all the technical skills and mastered all the musical instruments without effort, he did not cultivate the proper state of an artistic soul: solitude of spirit and a single-tracked passion. His master Cheng Lian said to him: I can teach you the skills of playing but am unable to change your temperament. Let me introduce you to my master in the East Sea and he will refine you. Cheng Lian took Bo Ya to the Penglai Mount in the Eastern Sea and abandoned him there. Bo Ya found himself to be the only soul in Penglai. Every day he heard nothing but the waves, the howling of the beasts, and the wailing of birds, until his mind was submerged in utter solitude. Only then did Bo Ya realize his teacher's intention. He plucked the strings of his instrument and composed the famous song, "Mind Cultivation of Narcissus."

More evidence of universalism in the human observation of nature and in thinking: Narcissus—the showy flower with a cup-shaped corona, a youth who fell in love with his own image in a pool, and who, after eventually pining away from unsatisfied desire—was transformed into the flower. Narcissism—self-love, egocentrism, erotic gratification derived from self-love. Therefore, genuine love is essentially love for the self. When Bo Ya finds Zhong Ziqi, his narcissism is satisfied. The sharer of the soul-music is the mirror image of the self. A true poet or any genuine being of artistic temperament must cultivate narcissism in order to achieve the wholeness of his soul. The realization of his achievement can only be proved by the other who is able to appreciate the musical flow of such a soul.

The friend who shares the music of your soul may not have to have sexual contact with you, but you and that person will achieve the highest exotic intensity and passion. A man seldom turns to a woman as a soul-mate (considering her unworthy of having a soul?) but feminizes another male or himself to copulate. One can even abandon the hope of finding such a friend among human beings. Lin Fu is an exemplar; he took plum blossoms as his wife and the cranes as his offspring—an ultimate realization of a person's narcissism through lifelong solitude. He transferred his autoeroticism into nature and enjoyed sexual rivalry with its denizens for the love of plum blossoms: "The sparse twigs of plum blossoms couch languidly in the limpid shallows of the river; Their subtle fragrance stirs the soul of the evening moon." Lin Fu had a phobia that roosters in the frosty dawn would steal looks at those plum blossoms ahead of him and dandy butterflies would seduce away their heart.

Yun decided to transfer her love to academic research, as she had succeeded doing in the past. But sexy Hawaii seemed to be the wrong place for such recuperation. The goddess of Hawaii is the volcanic Mount Kilauea that has taught its people the meaning of A-lo—ha and given them the handsign of "hang loose." For the first time she realized that the Dionysian eruption from the center of the earth—Mother Gaia—is not dangerous but magnificent. By its powerful overflow, Hawaii gains eight acres of land per year. Yun suddenly remembered that the continents had been formed by lava from volcanoes under the sea. Even if Mount Kilauea cooled into the snow-capped Rocky Mountains, the melting passions would still be inside. A few weeks later when Yun met Ramon, she gave him a lava ashtray in the shape of the sign "hang loose." When leaving she wanted to shake Ramon's hand, but he said: "We have passed that phase, haven't we?" Perhaps a man can; but a woman seldom passes a phase that is worthy of the name of true love. But, "Good-bye—because I love you."

On the Wings

" Welcome to America, pretty lady!" The customs officer greeted Yun aloud.

Pretty? Am I really pretty? All her life she knew that she was ugly and plain. Fortunately, she had been born in China at a time when women could surpass men through brain power and leadership. Many men nowadays learned to look up to women because of their qualities rather than their appearance alone. A pretty face on a woman showed bourgeois traits. A pretty face on a man was definitely disastrous, betraying sissiness and superficiality. Nevertheless, the customs officer's compliment titillated her. She felt a magic transformation occur from an ugly duckling into a swan. Its wings started fluttering in her heart. *Perhaps I am not that ugly.*

She saw the flashing figures on the electronic bulletin board: 13 August 1985.

ᐧᕁ   ᐧᕁ   ᐧᕁ   ᐧᕁ   ᐧᕁ   ᐧᕁ   ᐧᕁ   ᐧᕁ

A week ago. One afternoon when Yun was waiting for the bus to Qinghua Yuan, a young man crossing the street kept looking at her. Is he an acquaintance? No. She frowned and looked in a different direction. She squeezed into the bus only to find the young man right by her side. One stop, another stop, another. . . .

"Qinghua Yuan. Get off!" The conductor was rather rude.

She got off the bus. He did, too.

"Hi, my name is Du Ming. I'm a graduate of Qinghua University. "

"Oh, good. I came from Wuhan. My sister is living on the campus at Qinghua."

"I see. You are visiting your sister. Shall we take a walk

along the lake this evening?"

"Why?"

" Well, I just want to know you, to understand you."

She knew young men's tricks and always liked to cool them off at once. Wasn't being chased for being a woman an insult? *To know me as a woman, you must first know my substance.*

"You know I am well over thirty, already the mother of a child."

He did not show the disappointment she had expected.

It was getting dark. Someone knocked at the door. When her sister opened it, Yun saw it was he.

"Can we take a walk along the lake?" He looked straight at Yun. Her sister gave him an ugly look and shut the door.

At the Capital Airport.

"Ah, it's you."

"Where are you going?"

"America."

"I am going to study psychology at Princeton University." Du Ming gave a buoyant shrug. *Oh, I see. He put free love into practice even before getting on the plane.*

╫ ╫ ╫ ╫ ╫ ╫ ╫ ╫

Susan and Jim were waving to her as she passed the customs officer. Plain sailing, indeed.

"Can you guess what that officer called me?"

"A Chinese lady?"

"A pretty lady!"

"Why not? You are quite pretty." Both Susan and Jim assured her with sincere smiles. *Perhaps the American criteria for beauty are different from those of China. Perhaps, as Mencken perceives, the Americans have a libido for the ugly.* Yun was amused.

The following day Susan and Jim showed her around UC Berkeley. People with bald heads were chanting; a gypsy-like woman was blowing bubbles. Jim said she was a famous poet. A batch of young men spreading pamphlets reminded her of Red Guards. A middle-aged man was giving a partisan speech vehemently. Yun was not shocked because she had been to Hyde Park in London.

When she saw some black boys on Pier 39 acting like puppets

for money, she immediately tightened her vigilance—begging, a common scene in a capitalist country? No. She giggled to herself. She was not going to repeat the same mistake she had made in London, when a blond lady took a plastic spoon away with her food, Yun thought she was pilfering.

Jim stood in line for a large slice of pizza.

"The pizza on this pier is very famous. Look at this cheese."

The cheese stretched from his mouth to his hand like Chinese noodles. Yun felt that the image of pizza was unspeakable. A couple of years later, she got to know that pizza exemplifies vaginal power while the hot dog symbolizes phallic power, like the Washington Monument. Once her mouth had been assaulted by a masculine tongue in the office. Out of anger and comic sense, she wrote a vulgar verse.

> *A live Hot Dog*
> > *wagging its large tail*
> > *in a fleshy vault*
> *Clouds were choked in the mid-air*
> *Saliva of rain hung upon the cheeks*
> *Could a yin and a yang ever talk*
> *When Heaven was bitten by a*
> > *sleeping dog?!*

The following morning Susan, Jim, and Yun drove off before dawn, leaving eggs and meat in the refrigerator. Yun was concerned but Jim told her, "Never mind—food is cheap in America." Yun remembered that the American experts in Wuhan University were always complaining that they did not have enough food. But the cook said they left food almost untouched after each meal. Yun was then an interpreter. It took a while for her to convince the cook that Americans do not consider buns, rice, or any Chinese staple as food. For them, food means meat and greens. They eat rice like salt; a spoonful is quite enough for a day.

After breakfast in a country restaurant, the trip became more lively.

"Susan and I had lots of fun with students in China. You know Xue Ping. He told us he was making love with a girl on the playground every evening. What he really meant was talking or courting."

"You gave us a good laugh, too. During our first talk, you

told us your hometown was at the foot of Cock-crest Mountain," Susan added.

"What is funny about that?"

"You know what a 'cock' or 'balls' mean to Americans, don't you?"

Yun giggled. Although she had taught English in China for about eight years, she never knew the other meanings of those simple words.

"One colleague in our department taught a year in Beijing. You will meet him soon. He told us some funny stories. Susan, you tell her."

"The one about the Ming Tombs? Okay. Two Americans had studied Chinese for a few months and were ready to try it in the street. When they lost their way during a visit to the Ming Tombs, they asked two peasants, 'Qingwen, Shisan Ling zai nar?'

The two peasants looked at each other, stunned.

The two Americans thought their Chinese was not good enough. But as soon as they turned their backs, they heard the peasants saying, 'Isn't that strange? Their foreign tongue sounds just like Chinese, as if they were asking where the Ming Tombs are.'"

"Another tale is even funnier. One day an American was dining in a Beijing restaurant. He said something in English to the waiter. That waiter dropped a plate on the floor and fled. Can you guess what the matter was? The English words to that Chinese sounded like 'how long is your penis?' Yun, how do you say it in Chinese?"

So embarrassing. To say any words in English, even four-letter words, sounds natural; but it is too ugly to say them in Chinese. In a land congested with puritans, it was not surprising that when Americans teaching in China met, they resorted to entertaining themselves with sexy jokes. Chinese men love to entertain themselves by talking "dirty" sex. How about women? Yun did not know because she had never talked about that subject. But she heard the secretaries gossiping about Zhang San being a lord at home because her husband was impotent. In China, everybody knows it is taboo to talk about sex with the opposite sex. Talking is next to actually doing it.

"Chinese men look lethargic. What the whole nation needs is a sex drive."

Jim sounded like he wanted to poke China awake with a huge Western penis.

It did happen almost daily. Yun knew that Professor Huang's daughter married an American expert. A shocking scandal in the province. A humiliation to all Chinese maidens, as he was not only a foreigner but a twice-divorced man. Another, another, another. . . . The University simply did not allow female students to visit foreigners any more.

"Do you know Xiao Dong?"

"Yes. The most brilliant student in my class."

"He is here now."

"I know. His relative in America sponsored him to study history in America."

"That relative is Becky."

"Ah, she! The American graduate of my age? Xiao Dong is not quite twenty. Impossible."

"Yes. Anything in the world is possible. We foreigners in Wuda all know. Xiao Dong often stole into Becky's room."

"Becky told me that Chinese men are unenlightened in sex. But once they learn they are *great*." Susan sounded as though she had great admiration for Becky.

"Becky came to China with the sole purpose of finding a Chinese man. She used to have a visiting scholar from Beijing as her lover in the States. But that man was married and returned to China about a half-year ago."

"But Becky has a husband and she asked for an early return because of her mother's sickness."

Susan and Jim laughed aloud over the Chinese gullibility.

"Becky got back to the states and divorced her husband, a professor of philosophy. She and Xiao Dong are already married. Yun, you can make a phone call to your student. But don't let Becky know we told you about her."

About two years later, Susan and Jim divorced and each married a young student from a foreign country. Their colleagues in Wuhan made a big fuss. Why, Susan and Jim had been admired as the best-matched couple they had ever seen, a sharp contrast to the miserable, ill-yoked spouses in China.

=
2
=

Yun arrived in Edinboro on her thirty-fifth birthday. She often
heard people say she still looked like an undergraduate, around
twenty. Once a young student who wanted to be her boyfriend
made her feel embarrassed and ashamed of being so fraudu-
lently young to the foreign eye. She always liked to tell people
her age. *America is paradise for the youth. Everybody tries to
look young. Do you really want to be old?* She did not feel old,
anyway. In 1983, when she was studying comparative literature
in Shanghai, she found herself the oldest one in the whole class.
And she always stole to bed early for fear of burning out. Now
America had given her face another bout of acne—the beans of
youth, the Chinese say.

Yun was a lucky person, according to those who knew her.
In 1972, she was among the first of the work-peasant-soldier students to enter college. An old peasant had laughed, "Study
English? What's that to do with our learning from Dazhai?[1]
You'd better go abroad." His words earned Yun the nickname
"Liuyangde" (going-abroader). By and by nobody remembered
her real name any more. Then in 1976, she was recommended
to study English abroad, not because she was wise enough to vol-
unteer to be a peasant again after graduation, but because of her
fortune in being a fisherman while teachers of Wuhan
University and Henan University had fought fiercely for a
travel opportunity like two oysters. What could the Bureau of
Education do? They gave the opportunity to that country bump-
kin who would never dream of going abroad. That was when
Chinese leaders loved to create wonders. A peasant studying
English abroad was the eighth wonder of the world, wasn't it?

Then Susan and Jim came to teach for a year at Wuhan
University while Yun happened to be studying in Shanghai.
Once when Yun had dinner with them at the Peace Hotel, she
merely mentioned that she had been to Britain and she would
like to see America. As luck would have it, Jim's department
chairman heard that a brilliant Chinese lady longed to see

---

[1] Dazhai was a model in Chinese agriculture during the Cultural
Revolution.

America and offered her a teaching assistantship. Others lost twenty pounds studying to pass TOEFL or the GREs to get to America but she breezed into an MA program.

Yun was used to hard work. She even felt a loss if she did not try experiences like washing dishes, chopping vegetables, and carrying plates like other overseas Chinese students. Edinboro was a small university town. There were not many restaurants. However, her confidence and pleasant smile won her a job at the Edinboro McDonald's as its first non-American employee. She enjoyed working there and captured her pleasure, boredom, and pain in a long poem.

1

The warm air of McDonald's
          bellowing a greeting song.
I came to bathe myself
          in the team spirit of a crew of young.
I'm grilling the filet;
You're passing the nuggets;
She's dressing the D. L. T.;
He's taking up the Big Macs.
Mind your jargon: one drill on six.
"Thank you" and "Please,"
Your mouth should never sneeze.

We are as fresh as the tossing salad.
Beeping buttons and shrieking alarms forever
          keep us on the alert.
One to another as sweet as Danish,
Creating an atmosphere tastes like Vanilla
          creamy and rich.
When rush hour comes,
Every one is charged,
Like Chaplin in Modern Times
Plus Juggler's fingers.
When business is slow,
We recover ourselves from the robot role.
It's time to relax a little
And crack a few jokes.
What? You want me to teach you a bit?
You want to learn how to say

"I love you" in Chinese?
" Wo Ai Ni"—but do not say it
To every young Chinese girl you meet,
Or you'll get an indelible slap on your face
                    in the street.
Uproarious laughter drives dullness
        of having-nothing-to-do away.
The embarrassment of seeing a boy kissing a girl in public
        is no longer in the way.

I am awarded a "Speedee"
            for keeping the lobby neat.
I laugh at myself for unwittingly westernizing a homely
        saying "as clean as a hospital" into
            "as clean as McDonald's feet."
It is not strange to feel there are no strangers here;
Outlandish chat everybody is eager to hear.
Wherever I go, wherever I stay,
With a gluttonous smile,
The McDonald's Clown whispers to me:
Down to earth price
Fireside taste
Served with a cup of free team spirit.

                    2

There's a minute
        I was reciting Dickinson
            "How happy is the little stone"
A bird cautioned me:
        "Oh, stop! Your time is sold."

There's a moment
        I was watching
            red petals of catsup
                with golden mustard filaments
            a square yellow cheese carpet
                on minced green lettuce velvet
A severe eye whipped me:
        "Oh, stop! Your mind is sold."

Why my legs feel like an elephant
Why my mouth munches like a machine
Why my brain numbs like a tomb
The quick resembles the doom
A hush voice startled me:
            "Hush—stop all your inquisitiveness,
                 you know you are sold."

3

I watch the witch-pot of oil
            bubbling
I see the grill of Hell
            sizzling
I hear the nuggets singing
            a swan song
My heart is cleft by the toaster's
            long shrieking.

Why is your image so ugly?
Why is your vision so dark?
Why is your tone so mournful?
Why can't your mood be a lark?

If I have time to see the patterns of rose
If I have mind to hear the shades of Beethoven
If I can afford to chase the wind along the beach
If I am free to transcend all and each

Maybe I will be different
            Maybe Not.

Luckier still, an elderly lady who was the manager of a furniture store offered Yun a snug dwelling in her beautiful house. For free board, Yun would feed the dog, wash a couple of plates a day, and vacuum the house once a week. This seemed like no work for Yun at all. There was plenty of ice cream and meat to eat and so little to do. By Thanksgiving, Yun had already gained ten pounds. She started jogging like an American student.

When you are stuffed as a turkey
                    satiated like a cat
You want to curse yourself
                    or slap your mouth—
A lump of guilt and regret
wishing to turn into a laxative
But brooding on time only breeds a crab too pensive
An active slimming course costs you nothing expensive
                    just run—run—run
Around the track
                    one circle—another—another—
Sweat? —Oh, good
Out of breath? —Slow down
for a while—continue—run—run—run—
Run. . .
Till you feel utterly exhausted
Running is a mill
Grinding away all your fatty extra
Leaving only the quintessence you need for
                    a body of the acrobatic Spring and
                    a mind of a cucumber Summer Night.

A weight problem belongs to the privileged few in China, while in America it is a plague for many. But either in China or America "being slim" becomes a noose around the neck of young women.

╫ ╫ ╫ ╫ ╫ ╫ ╫ ╫

1982
A groaning came from the room next to Yun's, scaring her because it was the first time she had heard such a sound in real life. She pushed the door ajar and saw Lili sprawling on the floor, an alcohol bottle tumbling by her side. Horrible sight! Was it really Lili, a student of hers about four months ago? Yun recommended her as a teacher of English in Wuda for her glowing health and intelligence. Yun suddenly remembered the gossip that Lili was only eating an ounce of rice a day because she had been rejected by a man for "being too fat."

╫ ╫ ╫ ╫ ╫ ╫ ╫ ╫

Funny indeed—a man may be handicapped by his short

height and a woman by her weight. Song told Yun that girls in
Boston, unlike bumpkins in the Pennsylvania area, are very
slim. Why, if you are fat, you cannot even find a job there. Yun
thought if she were a boss, she would put "no weight discrimina-
tion" in the job ad. Nevertheless, Yun was neither slim nor fat.
A sort of gloating underlay her maxims such as "Choosing a
moderate diet shows the strength of self-discipline; starving for
the love of a man is losing oneself."

Yun's husband was extra-slim. Marrying someone you will
never love was another philosophy of hers. Yet, it was true that
she had never liked thin men.

My ancient girl
　　　　my ancient girl
What kind of man do you love?
I love a man with a mind
　　　　as broad as the word "tolerance"
I love a man with a heart
　　　　embedded with unblocked vessels of kindness
I love a man who is shape-blind
　　　　preferring the healthy plump to
　　　　　　the starved slim
I love a man who loves not for me or for himself

I'm no queen, he's no king
　　　　I am a fool
　　　　He is an idiot
We are safely locked in the
　　　　Casket of Mad marriage.

=

3

=

Hole-envy

After arriving in America, the first freedom Yun gained was being able to talk about sex.

Did Freud talk about a girl's envy for a penis? It was drizzling and Yun was thinking in her cubicle about what they had discussed in class. Perhaps there was something true in it. When Mei went to kindergarten at the age of three, for quite a while she refused to squat for a pee. She said other kids did not. She even tried to pee a rainbow, although she achieved nothing but wet pants. Yun laughed as she suddenly remembered a professor who had died while peeing an arc against an electric pole. Nevertheless, there was no evidence of Mei's envy for penis. When sexual difference became clear to her, she absolutely refused to act like a boy or wear boy's clothing.

"Are you willing to be reborn as a male in your next life, Mei?"

"No. You know, Mom, the three most brilliant kids in my class are all girls."

Once during an after-dinner chat, Jim said there was a "flasher" in this town of Edinboro. *What does that mean? Oh, a flasher is a naked man wearing a long coat who reveals his penis to women in a flash. I've never heard of such a pervert in China.* Actually, she had.

"Puritan," her roommate in Shanghai, was the most decent person Yun ever met; but from her Yun heard the most bizarre stories about the People's Liberation Army. One day a woman soldier was called to have a heart-to-heart talk with her platoon leader. Every word she heard was political jargon. When she lowered her head absentmindedly, she was shocked to see a huge penis flashing out of the open flap of the platoon leader's pants. What does this "flash" signify? A begging for a hole, isn't it? One PLA soldier was shot to death because he had poked a sheep which gave birth to a horrible creature during his troop's stay in a Tibetan area. Another soldier frequented a women's toilet at midnight, spraying semen into the sanitary napkin stained with menstrual blood. . . . So many male perverts.

Does anyone hear about female perverts? Yes. A woman died in Kaifeng putting a light bulb into her vagina. No woman would believe such a rumor. Moreover, a bulb was shaped more like an egg than a penis anyway.

Yun was trying to recall her first sight of a penis when George broke into the office. "Yun, have a piece of cake. Today is my birthday. I am twenty-three now."

"Congratulations! I am thirty-five. You young boys make me feel like a granny in the department."

George grinned at the free telling of her age and said, "We all love grannies. Truthfully, I love my granny at home most. I wish she could look as young as you. Hey, shall we have dinner together at the Golden Wok?"

"Why not? I'll give you a treat today."

Lately, the chubby George was quite emotional towards Yun, but Yun would not buy his sentiments simply because he was twelve years her junior. Yun seldom experienced equal communication with a man of her own age, let alone a sapling. Nevertheless, she loved George like a brother, and she sometimes secretly enjoyed an "incestuous" pleasure in the relationship.

Parting from George after dinner, Yun ran back to her cubicle. The rain was getting heavier. *What am I thinking?* She started scratching her confused thoughts in a poem she called "Electroencephalogram: A Birthday Tale."

it is the fading coal
the lingering image of a comet's bygone tail
your birthday is coming, not passing
today is your birthday—carpe diem
multifarious you keep popping up
the Hawaiian tourist
the dignified suit without a tie
no, not me.
you, the cherub
you, the infinite broadness
did i joke with you it's better to grow horizontally than
        miserly long as most men do
oh, a physical ode to generosity; gone with that scheming lean
Cassius
a woman could have married Caesar twice
ah, the sight of innocence

how you smile,   ripples of an autumn lake, endlessly soothing,
not enchanting
what a grieved look
even you, at your age, have internal fractures?
you are frowning,   still incapable of producing
                                          an aged wrinkle
who complimented you on your smooth cheese?
refuse to take me as your confidant—
all the better to imagine the wounds scarred or searing in a
child's heart
there must be a spiritual tie
is it that i want to draw some lifeblood for the child of my own
heart?
a noble theft, i hope, a nostril stealing fragrance

a little comic girl in a picture book
    puts her "calf love" in a tangible orange with a sisterly hand
how innocent of him to return a banana!
twenty or thirty years ago
her eyes first opened wild
looking at the difference in between an infant's snowy limbs
her hand holding a mouth organ in the shape of a cute yellow
banana
with two rows of tiny holes

are you really innocent?
what's so funny about eating a hot dog?
damn Freud
deprived us of illicit pleasure even in decoding the dream of a
pizza

wise to refresh the pretentious cubicle with profane chirpings,
eh?

on your birthday i wish you stop growing: be content
with being young, fresh, and knowledgeably innocent
with a postsophisticated brain
a primordial taste
medieval courtly manners

little brother
your elder sister may give you a birthday present
—only you guess it

priceless in the way it touches no tinge of money
but with a taint of imagination
it's the breath of breeze
it's the touch of the fleshy dawn
it's the warm ring of the setting sun
it's not from a male or a female
it's not the riddle of the Sphinx
it's perhaps labial but nonverbal

how i wish i could have an automatic imagination recorder in
my pocket
now nothing but a few crumbs gleaned

ha, Golden Wok
i'm watching you with your earphones on like a toy airplane
pilot
you chuckle
isn't this birthday tale amusing?

don't be annoyed by my wish that you stop growing
i know you contain no anger of the Tin Drum Boy
you'll grow to be David Ireland
the lover of leopards
not of kangaroos

how i envy the squirrels on campus—the true Greeks
mocking me?
shame on you, in and out of cubicles like a grave badger
tunneling through ages of pedantic rocks
whose new edges often cut my little fingers

what pleasure to watch
a lotus seedpod
green yet full of baby cherubs
rooted in the magnetizing silt
laden with freshness. . .

Her scribbling seemed to be endless. Accidentally, Yun saw the notice that a female graduate student in the English Department had been assaulted two days ago in the building. Even though Yun was strong enough to kick a man who lacks self-control the way Alima kicked Terry in *Herland,* it was wise for her to go home before eleven at night.

She ran all the way home like a mad woman. Soon she was standing under a shower. There were two criteria for testing the degree of a person's adaptation from China to America: taking a shower after bed or before bed; and dreaming in English or Chinese. Yun was still in the process of transition. In three months she had gotten gradually used to taking a shower in the morning. But today she was so preoccupied that she slipped into the old habit again.

The shower head was small but shaped like a huge penis and she found the water flowing down along the curves of her body and rushing into the hole under her feet. Where does the water flow? The heart of the earth, I hope. Rubbing soap around the edge of her own hole, Yun was thinking about why Long had been so curious about a woman's hole. Before their wedding Long begged her to let him see the mysterious hole. After their marriage, he was, perhaps, too excited to insert his power into that hole. He complained that there was no hole at all. Yun read about stone women in classical Chinese tales. Perhaps she happened to be one. They went to the hospital and the doctors laughed for she was still a virgin. She was not mad at Long because he had promised to be with her all her life even if she was a stone girl. *Why had he suggested that I have a contraceptive ring before leaving China?* Of course he did not trust her chastity that much, nor did she herself. Long also mentioned that a long spousal separation was not too difficult for a woman to bear. *What did he mean?* She smiled. A woman has ten fingers. Does a man has his own hole to release?

╫ ╫ ╫ ╫ ╫ ╫ ╫ ╫

1981

"Hey, I read something from the encyclopedia about Freud today. Do you know anything about him?" Xiao Fan was riding on a rusty bike. Xiao means "young" or "little" in Chinese. Actually Fan was well over fifty, almost the eldest in the department. Everybody called him Xiao Fan, because he was most knowledgeable and never wore out his childlike inquisitiveness.

"I heard something about him in Britain." Yun was riding a shining Five Goats, a lady's bike.

"Above all the talk about ego and id, to put it simply, Freud simply means that the sexual drive is like a man anxiously looking for a toilet. Nobody can really repress sex."

1973

"Hereby, I announce the decision of the university. Feng and Shen are expelled from the university because they made illicit love defying our repeated disciplines. . . ." The voice of PLA Representative Wang was decisive.

╫   ╫   ╫   ╫   ╫   ╫   ╫   ╫

"You know Representative Wang is going back to the army tomorrow?"

"What for?"

"He forced Feng to have sex with him when she was found having an affair with Shen. He threatened her: Do it with me or be expelled from school. . . ."

1977

"Hui and Ping are being sent back to China tonight."

"Why? We are allowed to study in Britain for two years. Not a year passed yet."

"Oh, you are still in the dark. Ping was caught fondling Hui's breasts the other night by Mr. Zhang."

1984

"Lian, how come your hair is turning gray and your neck has become so thick?"

"I feel more angry than shameful. Yes, we made love several times behind my husband and his wife. But I cannot understand why I am being punished by teaching in a lower place while he is not."

Lian continued, "Can you believe what the Chair said to me? He said, If you want to have an extramarital affair, why not with me?"

╫   ╫   ╫   ╫   ╫   ╫   ╫   ╫

Yun was still shocked when she recalled that conversation. That Chair had been Yun's secret admirer. She could hardly believe he was that cheap. A man is looking for a hole, no matter where it is located.

Boredom wrapped over Yun's warm, lazy body. She went to bed almost senselessly. The following morning she could not bear the sight of that phallus-like shower head and her host was kind enough to buy a new one, shaped like a sunflower. Yun was inspired by the new sight and new experience.

> *A peacock's tail*
> *A phoenix's trail*
> *A crystal chandelier*
> *A screen of silver beads threaded with golden hair*
>
> *It fans over your perspiring body*
>   *like a palm of feathers*
> *It caresses your lonely face*
>   *like a mother's gentle finger*
> *It admires your naked shame*
>   *with a thousand watery eyes*
> *It patters on the string of your worn-out nerves*
>   *like a wondrous seven-star needle[2]*
>
> *In ecstasy*
>   *you become the hub of a white chrysanthemum*
>   *pedaling its willowy petals*
> *In despair*
>   *acid tears join the streams*
>   *rushing over your body*
>   *empty into the sea through the sink*
>
> *Throw back your hair, flying as a swallow*
>   *greeting the sun-rays*
> *Tiptoe your feet, swirling as a petrel*
>   *dispersing the rain*
> *Stretch your arms and lean against the wall*
> *Watching a bunch of nails fix you on the cross*
>
> *How painful it is*
> *How blissful it is*
>   *to hail the rebirth*
> *In a shower of metaphors*
> *Metaphoricity of shower.*

Another month passed. Not a soul spoke Chinese to her. She must be forgetting her mother tongue. Do you ever dream in English? I don't know. But that night she had a significant dream.

---

[2] The seven-star needle is also called plum-blossom needle. It is used in Chinese acupuncture for curing many nerve problems.

I was talking to a Chinese colleague
　　　　who knows no English
I chattered and giggled, muttered and chuckled
　　　　he looked puzzled
　　　　　　dumb like a fool
I suddenly realized what a fool I am
　　　　I was speaking English
I made a conscious effort and switched to
　　　　Chinese
Another minute I lost my conscious control again
　　　　I was mumbling in English
The listener protested
　　　　I swerved to Chinese
　　　　　　with a screeching sound
Then I slipped to English again
My acquaintance disappeared
　　　　　　like a stranger
Like a stranger I was left in monologue alone
I did not know when
I did not care
I was, head over heels, shuttling between
　　Beckett and Nabokov, Nabokov and Beckett
When the alarm clock rang.

=
4
=

Time weighed heavily on her.   Idleness made her into a dreary hermit.   Fall gradually vanished with withering yellow leaves.   Winter came with dancing white flakes.   Yun was jogging slowly along the street in the evening.   She was stopped by the beautiful scene and had a momentary pleasure:

> *Crystal-knit maple branches—*
> *ice-woven webs*
> *A snow-hugged ridge—*
> *blown away white clouds.*
>
> *Boundless is my pleasure.*

Yun knew she was merely simulating that boundlessness. Life is full of boundaries and so are human emotions.   But an active life is just a process of breaking up states—material, spiritual, and emotional.

She stopped jogging at the intersection of the main street through the downtown area.   She was convinced of the coming of Christmas.   All the trees were decorated with lights and even street lamps were changed into septangular stars.   Suddenly street lamps were lit up.   She gazed upon one image until her soul merged into it.

> ***I AM***
> *a seven-petaled snow flower*
> *bearing the configurations of the heaven*
> *multiply as if in a kaleidoscope*
> *weaving the velvety patterns of*
> *a quilt*

beneath
I copulate with the root of wheat
penetrating with no protuberant organ
but soft fluid
to make man pregnant with seeds
while I'm happily vanishing. . .
rising with inaudible clouds
to the moon

where I crystallize patterns again with
nothingness in stillness
till another fall
to the earth.

Back at the house she found her only company—her shadow—more visible in the bright light. Mrs. Shirley had flown away to join her children and grandchildren in her ex-husband's residence in San Diego. Yun filled a bowl with dog food and opened the side door. She put the bowl outside and instantly withdrew her hand as if she had been bitten by a snake. She heard how Americans love dogs and some prefer dogs as their life companions. This German shepherd was too fierce for her. She read about a lonely lady who made TV into a substitute lover. Yun could not do that, either.

Yun got to know two other Chinese graduate students outside her department: Hong majored in education and Ping was in library science. Hong's baby was only two months old when she left; Ping's boy was no more than three, and Yun's girl was about six. How they laughed when they first met, not only because their husbands had to take care of kids like moms, but also because the men's bikes were simultaneously stolen in spite of the fact that one was in Wuhan, one was in Xi'an, and one was in Shanghai. A bike in China, like a car in America, is a person's extended legs. They were truly grounded at home.

Now Hong went to New York to stay with an old Australian professor who had sponsored her to America. Ping went to Pittsburgh to work in a restaurant since she did not have financial aid. Jim went away to join Susan in Spain. There was not even a soul to call. For the first time loneliness soaked into her marrow.

Actually a modern person's loneliness in a crowd is very much a personal choice. Jeff first invited her to go to Florida with him. She declined, but Rose went. An admirer of hers kept calling her every week and asked her to rent a room for him in Edinboro so that he could come and visit her from Iowa. When Yun mentioned this to Jim, Jim laughed, "That snarling cat; tell him to walk to Edinboro." Last week when the Iowa cat joked that he could not wait to slap her butt, Yun had had enough of his vulgarity.

The following evening was Christmas Eve. Christmas was an occasion for family reunion like the Chinese Nian (New Year). What is the Nian? A horrible beast. All of the Chinese have an orgy on the eve of Nian's coming, because they know that there will not be any tomorrows. They will all become ex-crement in the belly of Nian. Nevertheless, Nian never comes. The Chinese still indulge themselves in merry-making but the meaning has changed. Nian means New Year, the beginning and re-beginning of time, space, memory, love, hatred, re-venge. . . .

As the Chinese saying goes, a festival doubles a person's nostalgia and longing. Did she miss her parents? Yes, but not that keenly. A married daughter is like water poured out-side—no longer belonging to the family. Meng, her ex-lover, al-ready remarried. A speck of pity for him, a man who had strug-gled for almost twenty years to free himself from the coffin of a marriage and had now fallen into another one. Someone said Meng still looked tortured, like the man in Kafka's *Trial,* after he fulfilled the ordinary Chinese male's dream of marrying a nurse-secretary. Yun should lawfully miss her husband Long, an honest, dependable man. Long means "dragon" in Chinese. She tried hard to think of him sweetly and even thought of writ-ing an ode to the Silent Dragon. But the inspiration refused to come. The dream she had last night was perhaps truer than her conscious thoughts.

> *Oh, what a dream!*
> *I ran here and there*
>   *I searched the cupboard*
>   *I looked between the linen sheets*
> *I am so free*
>   *I have no link with anybody.*
> *Am I married?*
>   *Where's my husband?*
>   *Who's my husband?*
> *Bliss? Fear?*
>   *Wandering in pondering. . .*

> *Ah, there he came*
> *or rather, I found him*
> *I found him calm, serene, emotionless*
> *and motionless*
> *We were jointed silently in candle taste.*

Yun twisted her mouth. Though the candle was hard to chew she bore it willingly. During those years of flowers and butter-flies, Jiang broke her heart and she broke at least three men's hearts, although not out of gender revenge. Feng wrote her a poem each week for three years and he was almost killed in a train crash during a special trip to see her. Yet, he lost her to a slight shortage of confidence and patience. When Yun finally wrote a letter responding to his love, he was already married. His bride mocked him as "an abandoned orphan" at their wed-ding. But he still worshiped Yun as the moon. Her second suitor was nicknamed "True Man" in the department. He was dark and tall, quite macho looking.

╫   ╫   ╫   ╫   ╫   ╫   ╫   ╫

1974

"Hey, look at the 'True Man' at the foot of the building. He has been staring at our window for days."

Yun looked down and saw Chang's dazed look.

Chang had behaved very strangely towards her lately. One moment he was trying unsuccessfully to tell her a joke. Another moment he was asking for some sort of silly help. Yun felt threatened by his masculinity.

The following noon Yun's best friend Qin asked her to take a walk with her along the lake. She sounded very mysterious. Qin finally told her that Chang had asked her to ask Yun whether she could be his girlfriend. Yun was already 24, theo-retically mature about that delicate human relationship. Moreover, she had been class president for the past two years. So she talked with Chang directly.

"What do you know about me?"

Silence.

"How old are you?"

"Twenty-two."

"See, you're two years younger than me. In addition, our personalities seem to be very different . . . ."

"Are you going to inform on me to the department?"

"Why should I?"

╬   ╬   ╬   ╬   ╬   ╬   ╬   ╬

Yun thought she had handled the situation perfectly. Who knew that a True Man would never forgive a rejecting woman, however? The True Man started his war against the fair sex. He played with the emotions of a young faculty member and led her to a nervous breakdown. Then he set two first-year students at war for his so-called love. When he saw Yun talking to any man, he would spread many rumors about her.

The third suitor was that scowling cat. He was one of the first batch of master's candidates in Wuda. After Yun married, he audited her English class like a good student. He sometimes visited her at home and sometimes caught her in her daily walk around the playground. Whatever he did, he was wallowing in an unfulfilled dream. His visits made Long feel extremely un-comfortable. Yun never showed strong disgust toward him. Perhaps, being adored on a pedestal is a pleasant feeling for any being.

How could you marry Long? Yun had been asked this question hundreds of times by her acquaintances.

When Yun returned from England she was twenty-eight, already too old for men her age. Nevertheless, Yun was the only returned student in the whole province. Her uniqueness must have aroused some young men's attention. Several senior professors offered to be go-betweens. Yun interviewed one suitor after another, none to her taste. Intelligent but arrogant; honest-looking but stupid. . . . Professor Ma started to tease her. "Yun, don't be that choosy. Do you know bachelor Zhou's story? Twenty years ago he was a tall handsome young man and attracted a lot of girls. He interviewed one after another. If a girl was beautiful and lively, he thought she must be a flirting type; if a girl was quiet, he thought she must be too dumb. When he grew much older, he was determined to catch one, blindfolded. When the girl came with me to see Zhou, Zhou asked her, 'Have you seen any tigers in town?' The girl decided to marry me. Do you see my point, Yun?"

Yun was then sharing a room with a young faculty member in mathematics. She was about Yun's age but looked younger and prettier. She told Yun she had missed two young men in her life already. Now one suitor was worse than the previous one. If she married any one of them, the two men she had rejected would laugh in her face. Moreover, she had never felt passion for a man. Yun felt no great passion for any man either, but she was clever enough to see that a Chinese woman over thirty needs marriage to achieve greater freedom in public. The odd maids in her university were isolated in their cells for fear of hearing gossip such as "too ugly to attract a man," "too neurotic for a man," "too choosy—it serves her right," "a whore," "a slut," "a simpleton," "a stone woman," "a yin/yang creature." Most of them aged prematurely.

Being a much more practical person, Yun listed all the suitors coolly like math problems and weighed each one's qualities. She set herself a deadline of two weeks to "solve the personal problem." She wrote a letter to her sister in Beijing. Her sister was shocked to see the list of suitors and wrote back. "You have changed much after your stay abroad. I found the leftist image of you two or three years ago much more lovable." That helped Yun make the final decision. She refused all the suitors and married Long for his simplicity, honesty, and dependability. Oh, God—what she had suffered for her free choice.

She started reviewing old mail. In a letter her sister said, "As I saw from the very beginning, you and Long are an ill-matched couple." What an irony. She scanned all the letters from Long. There was not even one word of love or about missing her. Every sheet was laconic, like a business telegram. Once she had asked him whether he loved her and he retorted, "Can you see?" Yes, he cooked three meals a day for her. But she could not tolerate him being mute like her mother.

To help overcome her sadness, she took out Mei's picture, which had been taken at the Beijing Zoo before she left the country. Mei was so cute riding on a pony; her expression was naughty and dreamy just like her mother. But when Yun set her eyes on the Mei's picture recently sent by Long, Yun's tears began to stream. She could not believe that the expressionless, dull little thing was her Mei. Even a child could not be growing healthily in a place with an unlighted lamp.

Thinking of the child, her mood brightened a little. She released a sigh of comfort. If I have accomplished nothing in academics, I have produced a child—the masterpiece of a woman.

1980

"Two fingers wide."

"Four fingers wide."

The nurse who had shaved her was measuring with her

eyes. With scissoring pain, Yun could almost hear the unbuck-
ling of the riblets at the entrance of her womb.

"Please, give me a Caesarean operation and let it out. Ah. .
.ah. . .ah. . . I am dying. . . ." The nurse cast an indifferent eye
on her. She must have seen countless mothers crying and
moaning like this.

Yun was tortured in hell for the whole night. When dawn
came, the nurse finally announced, "Her hour has come" and
wheeled her to the delivery room.

The actual birth was pretty easy. The baby came headlong
out almost by itself, just as her mother said later, "When a
melon is ripe, its butt falls by itself."

After all, having a child was easy. Yun was lying in bed, almost forgetting the throes of birth. Marrying at 28, she was a
model for late marriage. Before the wedding she made her husband agree that they would not have any children for three
years. But after five or six months, Yun felt a yearning for a
child, like a call deep from the ravine in her body, so Yun and
Long stopped using contraceptive means. But Yun simply could
not get pregnant. There must be something wrong with one of
them, most likely Long since he looked vulnerable. Long
thought it was his fault, too, and said that if Yun wanted a divorce, they could get one. Yun was moved: "Let's be happy together without children."

Then, all of a sudden, Yun had strange symptoms, as though
she was hungry all the time but food could not cure the eagerness
or sourness of the body. By the time she was diagnosed as pregnant, her morning sickness was gone. "Believe me, my baby
never stopped me one minute from working," Yun used to brag.
But it was quite true. She was never absent from teaching; the
water began to flood her pants when she graded the last of the
final examinations.

The ward she stayed in was huge, containing at least eight
new mothers. For twenty-four hours a day, the noise inside
boomed like a cinema. Since she was immobile, Yun could only
get acquainted with the two patients on either side of her.

The woman on her right had twin girls. In a minority national region a mother giving birth to twins would be burned to
death as a witch. Never mind, we Han people love twins, particularly girls—one mirroring the beauty of the other. I have one
baby. But all babies look alike; the nurses could make a mistake about whose is whose. Also, somebody could deliberately
swap babies. Yun was tense for a minute and relaxed with a

smile. So what, babies are born equally new. It really does not matter whose is whose.

"Why, the lady on my left is already gone! Did the doctor say a mother must stay in the hospital for three days?" Actually, why not go home? Yun remembered her mother tumbled out of the delivery bed and cooked dinner for the whole family.

"She is too ashamed to stay here. Her baby was born with a birth defect; it has a large transparent spot through which one can see its intestines. The young couple escaped without taking their baby. "

Good heavens! What does my baby look like? It may have six fingers on a hand, or holeless in the bottom, or . . . . Yun was tense and then relaxed again. No matter how it is, it is my flesh and blood. I must keep it. I must keep it.

Yun was lucky. Her baby was perfect, almost too beautiful. People say monthlings should be ugly; only ugly monthlings grow into great beauties.

╫ ╫ ╫ ╫ ╫ ╫ ╫ ╫

A card fell to the floor. Picking it up, Yun saw it was the only Christmas card from China. The strokes of the characters were familiar. No doubt, it was Meng's handwriting, Meng, now Chair of the Chinese Department at Wuda. Yun felt waves of sadness. Meng used to be Yun's semi-secret lover in China. Their relationship was semi-secret because they were bold enough to associate with each other openly but nobody was really sure about whether they had had an illicit affair. The fact that they had never been caught spoke for their innocence. Nevertheless, they had made love once.

In late 1984 Chinese lovers' activities were still being monitored. Ming and Hua were caught and humiliated by the whole campus; Songli did not get a promotion because he had had an affair with one girl but attempted to marry another one; Meng was toppled from his position simply because of his struggle for a divorce and his close association with Yun.

Yun had been puritanical, but the tyranny of public opinion angered her and turned her into a rebel. She was more touched by the last scene of Qingwen and Baoyu than ever before in the *Dream of the Red Chamber*.[3] Then Yun's husband was at the

---

[3] In the *Dream of the Red Chamber*, the innocent maid Qingwen is accused of seducing her young master Baoyu and is persecuted. Before her death, as a defying act, she bites off her fingernails and gives them to Baoyu and exchanges her inner garment with his.

University of Beijing for a year of advanced study. One night she pushed a graduate student out when he attempted to assault her in her apartment. The following night she invited Meng to come over and they made love. Why does a woman reject one and take another? That graduate student was younger and had a much more attractive body. But Yun made what she would consider to be a political gesture, an act of willful defiance.

Yun and Meng were peers rather than lovers. They collaborated in some research activities. Yun had more time and always did more but when it came to publication, they became resentful towards each other. Meng did not want to place his name behind Yun's because he was a man and her senior. Finally, they had to use a two-character pen name and each character suggested one person—a significance shared between them only. But one could not say there was no love between them. In the mornings Meng jogged a long circle to watch Yun shadow box on the basketball grounds; one night after a school meeting, Meng went to sit by her in the cinema when the film was almost over; and Yun had created all sorts of academic excuses just to see him in the small room he shared with his big son, a humane boy. When his son reached the age where he missed having a girlfriend, he said to Yun that her relationship with his father was admirable.

But Yun and Meng did not really talk much about love. Meng's praise of a woman's feminine virtues often upset her stomach. When Meng talked about people's gossip about them, he would say, "If we marry each other, we will become too strong for the department." The men of the department, perhaps sensing the coming threat, had tried to stop them in every way.

The summer before Yun went to America, Yun and Meng taught night school together. When they were bicycling home in the darkness, Meng always liked to ride ahead, calling back to her: "Follow me!" "Who follows whom" had indeed been the focus of the rivalry between the two of them. Meng succeeded in obtaining his divorce but Yun could not marry him. Like Cowherd and Weaving Maid,[4] they were eternally separated by the Pacific Ocean. Three years later, Yun received a call from Meng, who was visiting Columbia University. He said his second marriage was not happy. Well, he had married a nurse-sec-

---

[4] In the Chinese folk tale, Cowherd married the fairy Weaving Maid. When the Weaving Maid was forced to go back to heaven by the Queen Mother of the Western Heaven, Cowherd chased behind her with their two children. But Queen Mother eternally separated Cowherd and Weaving Maid by drawing a Milky Way with her hairpin between them.

retary and gotten back his position of Chair, which led to his full professorship. What else did he desire?

Examining the official card again, Yun remembered that she had sent Meng a personal card upon her arrival in America. She did not write a word but the card was designed with a thousand words of "love." They each failed to conquer the other. His pet phrase of "Follow me" buzzed in Yun's ears until she jotted down a few lines.

> *The sun was bright*
> *How I admired his height*
> *I beheld his motion lovingly*
> > *in my maiden sight*
> *He asked, "Would you follow me?"*
> *I walked silently*
> > *side by side*

> *The moon was beautiful*
> *Said the burning sun*
> > *holding all things below*
> > > *with his golden threads*
> *" Would you follow me?" he invited*
> *She circled him pondering*
> > *in equal distance of light*
> > *Not behind*
> > > *nor ahead*

> *The sun says he knows no wane*
> *The sun says he sheds no rain*
> *The sun says he has no black holes*
> *"Follow me!" he commands*
> *"No! I prefer to wander alone"*
> > *faded out the Blue Moon*
> > *No front*
> > > *nor back.*

Yun's thinking glided from Meng to Jim. Jim seemed to be a surrogate for Meng. Yun was more attracted to him than to Meng because of his sensitive temperament. But Yun and Jim were not equals—he was her sponsor, advisor, and professor, while she had stepped down from the comfortable position of a faculty member to the plight of a struggling foreign student.

While Yun often reminded herself to be grateful to Jim, she had an irresistible tendency to resist him. After Susan left for Spain, Jim once asked Yun to go to Pittsburgh for a weekend. Yun declined. When she told Mrs. Shirley about it, the old lady said rather disappointedly, "Why refuse him? He got you here from China, didn't he?" Then Mrs. Shirley laughed, "Jim was born in the month of the scorpion. I can tell he's a horny man. Well, when I was young, I never minded going to bed with my boss."

Yun felt that she was being punished—she had to feed Jim's dog daily during his absence. The autumn storm in Pennsylvania was furious. Her umbrella had blown over twice. While desperately folding the tearing umbrella, she fell and hurt her knees badly. The night that Jim was leaving for Spain, Yun went to his house to say goodbye. They talked intimately but always with tiny pullings of resentment. One moment Jim seemed to be aroused by Yun, and asked, "Do you like fondling the body a little?" Yun knew perfectly well what he meant but pretended not to understand him. She soon regretted not having gone along with him, because she felt the same desire. They finally shook hands in a comradely fashion and parted.

Now on this lonely Christmas, Yun was thinking of him acutely and lovingly, because he was away.

> *Hate is close and tense*
> *Love, remote and dreamy,*
> *   has beauty immense*
> *Lukewarm is a slimy shore*
> *Indifference cataracts the eyeball—*
> *Seeing is no-seeing just as before.*

Between Yun and Jim were feelings of love, hatred, resentment . . . But they could never become indifferent to each other. The foundation of their friendship was solid because of their mutual caring. She sent him a Christmas card with the words:

> *A card?*
> *No. A feather*
> *Flying over a thousand miles*
> *To greet you on Christmas*
> *Light, the present*
> *Deep, the feelings*

Sweet, the heart
From a friend
As near as your presence
As distant as the ocean cliffs.

Yun did not will herself to sleep that night. She fell asleep when her brain lost its conscious function. She opened her eyes to a ray of sunshine from between the curtains. The snow had stopped. *Well, what shall I do today?* She had so much time and so little to do. She put on her boots and ambled to the campus library. It was open but hardly a soul was inside. She went to the magazine section and met a professor from the education department. Her name was Cynthia. Her sharp features showed her to be a woman of intelligence and willfulness. They chatted for a while and then Yun went with her to her house nearby for tea. Cynthia had a four-bedroom house that she had just bought for herself; it had a study, sewing room, painting room, and sleeping room with a queen-sized bed. Coming from an over-populated world, Yun felt guilty occupying too much space, never dreaming she would one day have a house. She was always content with a studio. She read, wrote, typed, exercised, and slept in the same room. She also liked a huge bed, with her books, papers, and dictionaries spread over half. She was a clean person, but messy. Everything was so convenient in her own messy way; she would lose track of her things when they were tidied up.

Cynthia served high tea in the style that Yun had become familiar with in Britain.

Munching little biscuits and sipping hot tea, they talked.

"Do you live in this house all by yourself?"

"Yes, I like to be by myself."

"Never married?"

"Well, I was married some years ago. But I divorced my husband."

"Because he was not faithful to you?"

"Not at all. I divorced him in order to make him independent. He was a weak man and relied on me for everything like a child on his mother. After we divorced he was forced to stand up in the world. He married another woman and has two children now. We have always been friends, now better friends, as he has finally grown up in emotion and responsibilities."

"Do you still see each other."

" Well, occasionally. His wife and children are quite demanding."

"How about yourself? Are you going to marry again?"

"Not really. I'm over forty now. In this country a woman of my age can hardly attract a man of similar age and intelligence. Men like to marry younger women. It's universal, isn't it?" Cynthia betrayed a hidden sadness.

Cynthia seemed to be talking not about her former husband, but about Yun's. If loneliness was the fate of one who set free a spousal dependent, Yun was not going to do it. She was selfish, incapable of setting a man free at the expense of annihilating herself.

When spring came, Mrs. Shirley asked Yun to move out. Yun was surprised because they had been getting on well, like daughter and mother. Before Yun came, Mrs. Shirley only had spells of sleep, for fear of burglars; now she snored soundly every night. Before Christmas, their phone rang constantly. Each time they picked up the phone, however, there was no response. One night a man rang their bell, delivering a pizza they had not ordered. Yun saw Mrs. Shirley break into tears. Yun learned that a young worker in Mrs. Shirley's office was attempting to take over her position by playing tricks on the old lady. At other times Mrs. Shirley would read Yun's applications to universities. The wisdom she passed to Yun was "Dare to sell yourself." When Mrs. Shirley was deserted by Mr. Shirley, she had established herself as a saleswoman. She had not gone to college but everybody around thought she had a PhD. Well, she was not poorer than any PhD in her job anyway.

"Why are you driving me out?"

" Well, you are not a considerate person. You have stolen my son from me. Every time Tim comes, he talks with you as though I do not exist in this house."

Yun remembered Mrs. Shirley's wistful looks when Yun had make-up on, ready to go out. And she recalled a conversation with Jim not long after she had gone to live with Mrs. Shirley.

"Yun, I saw Mrs. Shirley today. Can you guess what she told me? She thinks there's something going on between you and her son Tim. Yun, you do not like that type of feminine man, do you?"

Actually, Yun liked feminine men more than macho men. She was somewhat attracted to Tim. But it was a pleasant, harmless attraction between a man and a woman. It was like getting on the train and being attracted by a passenger of the opposite sex, but parting from one another easily at one's own destination. Once a letter from a train passenger, a young intellectual from Suzhou, had been forwarded to her. His letter told Yun that he was so impressed by her personality that he tried to find her at her university. Nevertheless, he did not know her name correctly and did not even know which department she was in. It must have been like searching for a needle in the sea. Refusing to give up, he took a train to Nanyang, Yun's hometown. Without knowing her street number, he lived in a hotel for three days waiting for a miracle to happen. When the letter finally reached Yun, she felt flattered. But that man did not even leave his address in the letter. What each person gained is a beautiful memory.

Tim was obviously attracted to Yun. When he was shopping with his mother and Yun, he would forget some of the items on the list his wife had given. In the past he seldom visited his mother. Now he visited two or three times a week. Yun knew nothing would really happen between her and Tim. It would be just a pleasant memory of attraction. The mother was obviously jealous. Freud had explored a son's love for the mother but failed to give enough attention to a mother's sexual need for the son.

1985

One day Ying dropped in, crying before she could say a word. To Yun's surprise, Ying had aged overnight, with visible gray hair. What had happened? She was only twenty-seven, a young lady who loved singing and laughing.

"Yes, something terrible happened but nobody will believe that it did."

"Don't cry. Tell me—I will believe you."

"My mother-in-law came to see us two weeks ago. You know we only have one room and one bed. So at night my husband Gang would sleep on my left side and his mother on my right. About a week ago I was half awakened at midnight by the movements a married woman is familiar with, you know, on my left side. I thought Gang was masturbating but when my arm accidentally touched my right side, it was vacant. I was fully awake by then but too scared to pull the light string. So I lay there quietly, heard his mother climb down from her son, use the night pan, and then return to her side of the bed. I felt so wretched that I did nothing but weep during the next days.

When Gang asked me what had happened, I felt too horrible to mention it. When I finally told him the truth, he accused me of being mad. When I told our unit leaders, they all regarded me as a mad woman, having hallucinations. . . ."

"I believe what you said is true. According to Freudian theory, sexual love between mother and son is quite possible."

Upon hearing that a theory supported her, Ying calmed down.

"Now that I think about their relationship, I recall many clues that Gang gave me early on. Gang said his father died young and that he most resembles his father among all her children. So his mother loves him best. Once he was in the hospital and his mother held his penis to help him pee. He and his mother see each other twice a year. If he is not going to Wuhan to visit her she comes to see us. I begged Gang not to associate with her anymore. He felt insulted. It would have meant admitting that there was something between him and his mother. What should I do now?"

" Well, you may get a divorce. You complained several times that Gang always takes liberties with young girls at school. I think that is a worse behavior than being intimate with his mother as a gesture of sympathy for her. "

"He knows a secret about me. I told him that when I was seventeen years old, I was raped by a man."

"That was not your fault and that is over. "

"That man did it more than once or twice. He did it to me whenever he had an opportunity. "

"What do your parents think about Gang's abnormal behavior?"

"They do not support our divorce. My father wants me to keep it to myself."

Yun had a slight suspicion that the man who had frequently abused Ying was her own father. She knew Ying wanted to hear "Be quiet, then. Perhaps human beings have to compromise in order to live together." But she said firmly, "If I were you, I would get a divorce."

╫ ╫ ╫ ╫ ╫ ╫ ╫ ╫

Mrs. Shirley's son sent Yun to a new host family. They both felt bad. There were not even pleasant memories to cherish anymore as they had been torn by a mother's feelings.

=
5
=

Yun was lucky to live with the Greens—a happy, healthy, typical American family. The word "typical" perhaps was incorrectly used; it only reflected how Yun felt. In fact, Mrs. Green, or Meggy, said she would never change her citizenship from Canadian to American. She sometimes fought with Mr. Green about American politics.

Meggy was a marvelous woman, well-balanced among her roles of woman, mother, and wife. She wanted to have Yun move in because she was working on her master's degree and too busy to take care of the house. She was preparing to enter a doctoral program. Mr. Green marveled several times, "I have no idea how she got grants and loans to start her education when Chris got to elementary school." They had three children; the eldest daughter, thirteen, was a beauty from a fairy tale; their second daughter was a cute girl with a generous nature just like her mother; Chris, the youngest child, was a gifted son. As soon as Yun stepped into their house, Chris asked, in the manner of a scholar, "Why do the Chinese use chopsticks? And why do pandas eat bamboo?"

Meggy liked to chat and laugh with Yun. She said Mr. Green looked better when he reached middle age—Yun understood that in her eyes Mr. Green had once been lanky and ugly. Meggy had loved an army officer. Every time she saw him, her body would be trembling. Her love for that man was just too much. But when Mr. Green drove all the way from America to Canada to see her, she knew they were going to get married.

"Any happy marriage has to be living and growing. The wedding is just the beginning. Both sides have to keep their creativeness for romance in life; otherwise, marriage will become stagnant and miserable." Yun loved to listen to Meggy's little theories.

Meggy was not only saying but practicing them. No matter how busy she was, she would remember to invite Mr. Green to a good restaurant, or a movie, or the beach. When they were away for a romantic time, Yun would babysit. Actually, the children were all self-reliant and they never needed any help from Yun, who was merely there to make the children feel safe. When Meggy returned, she would give her children a treat at McDonald's. The children loved that. They wished their parents would leave them alone more often.

The Greens were a sociable family. They liked to invite friends over for the weekend or dinner and they often went out. The Greens and other faculty families in Edinboro had organized a gourmet club. They met monthly at different houses to eat, drink, and talk. When the Greens went they often took Yun along. At one party, after eating, people sat around talking about their first love. One said his first love was his nursery teacher; another said his was an elementary teacher; another said hers was a sick young boy in her neighborhood. When everyone else let the cats out from their hearts, people remembered Yun and urged her to confess her first love.

" Well, well, I do not know whether I fell in love with anyone before the age of twenty-four." Everybody laughed, including the kids. Some of the schoolchildren already had boyfriends or girlfriends.

At another party Yun saw Marie sitting with a young man. Marie kept stroking his thighs or nudging him affectionately and looked at him from time to time with lusty greediness. Meggy told Yun that the young man was Marie's husband, a student from Saudi Arabia, twenty-three years her junior. Yun remembered that while she was working at McDonald's, this young dandy had come in with two little kids; he was wearing flowery shorts like a big kid.

Marie was really something, Meggy said. When she wanted a child she simply had an affair with an officer in a barrack. Have you seen her child? A handsome boy. She married this dandy boy, defying all the public opinions. The boy was barely twenty, and only wanted money from her. She bought him a sports car and got him into a program at University of Pennsylvania. Of course she also rented an expensive apartment for him. Then every weekend, she would drive to Philadelphia to have a little romance. When she was not there, that boy was just hanging around with young girls on campus. Who expects him to study, anyway? One day a famous French scholar, a single man, was coming to give a talk in Marie's department and was to stay in her house for a couple of days. I thought Marie should develop a relationship with him. Can't you guess what? She drove all the way to get her dandy back and introduced him to that scholar while playing a most faithful wife.

In early May some friends from Peru and Brazil came to the Green's for a party. At the end of the party, a man from Peru hugged everybody goodbye. When coming to Yun, he stopped and shook her hand, perhaps because Meggy had introduced her as Chinese or because some uneasiness in her eyes stopped him.

Yun recalled a hug-disaster in her life. In 1977 when she was in Britain with a group of Chinese sent by the Chinese government, they were frequently invited by British leftists to their organized activities, due to the influence of Red China. Once their group was invited by the miners and steel workers of Sheffield to spend a weekend with them. They followed their hosts to attend a meeting. At the meeting the workers asked the Chinese students to sing a song. They sang "The five-star flag is fluttering; our song is soaring into the sky. . . ." Before the fall of the last musical note, a young worker came over to Yun and said her singing was beautiful, hugging her. Then the workers started to sing one song after another. They started with "We shall overcome. We shall overcome. . ." but pretty soon got around to singing love songs. Steven, a known British communist, was very angry with the workers and called them "the unenlightened" and the workers called him a "petty-bourgeois." The party ended unpleasantly. When Yun got back to London where she was studying, she was criticized by her group leader. He told Yun that Steven was shocked that a young man gave her a "big embrace" at the party. Yun protested, "The Embassy has told us that hugging is a Western custom. Moreover, he hugged me—it was not my fault." Nevertheless, when Yun returned to China, Meng told Yun that the Education Bureau in Beijing knew about her scandal in Britain—she was caught embracing her professor in public. Meng said that with a sinister smile as if every virtuous woman was a cracked egg, attracting flies.

Compared with people from Latin America, Yun felt deeply that the Chinese revolution had deprived the Chinese of physical touch, feelings, and love. Were her Chinese ancestors all puritans? Who said that in classical Chinese there was no character for "kiss" until the 18th century? Even if they did not record this crude human behavior, they did it all the same. Only the modern Chinese, born in new China and growing up beneath the red flag, had lost the tradition of love. Yun pondered the difference between the classical character and the simplified character of love.

> *I love the old Chinese character "Love"* 愛
> *for it has a heart of its own* 心
> *When the heart vanishes into pure friendship* 友
> *it becomes Platonic love* 爱
> *maybe too puritanical —*
> *it is part of me*
> *which is strangling me —*
> *bars of bone in the chest*
> *protect as well as jailbird the heart.*

Mr. Green, or Art, was also an interesting person. Apart from teaching in communications, he loved wood carving. Yun said, "Art is wonderful, giving eternal wings to the shriveled and bringing delicate beauty out of wooden ugliness." Art had an MA in English literature and they had a lot to talk about. One day, Art showed Yun a collection of poems by his friend T. E. Porter. Yun read them with interest and translated them into Chinese overnight. The translating added wings to her already awakening poetic sensitivities. She could chant almost anything into a poem. The Greens' white cat passed her. She said the "cat" was really fat; Meggy said her pronunciation of "cat" sounded like "kite." Well, cat—kite.

> *Though I have wings*
> *though I can fly*
> *higher than a sparrow*
> *almost out of sight*
> *yet to an invisible string*
> *to the ground I am tied—*
> *soaring like an eagle*
> *Nothing but a Kite.*

Jim told Yun that Edinboro should only be a gate for her to America. As soon as her wings were strong enough she should fly to a larger university. Yun applied to University of Illinois because it did not require an application fee. Like those penniless students from mainland China, what Yun was really seeking was financial aid. She felt like a mute, begging in America.

There's something I do not have the courage to ask
on the phone
but I have the audacity to write
There's something I cannot give
in person
but I can send day and night

There's something in me
that is mysterious and desperate
—wild, wild
like prairie fire
burning—burning—burning. . .

There's something like a baby
clapping its hands and
kicking its feet
in my cerebral womb
There's something like embryos of seeds
bursting off their skin
ready
to shoot and boom

There's something like a voice above
cracking a battle-cry:
It's time to gather your wild geese
in black and white!

But my Pedestal or Guillotine:
Can I succeed
with a tongue I do not know
how to twist
under the scraping of Time and Money's blade?

The weather was getting hot and the semester came to an end. The Greens were driving to Vancouver for a month-long vacation. When the family were shouting a goodbye to her, she had the feeling that she would not be able to see them anymore. Seeing Art, the self-labeled Nobody, driving a van of cheerful faces off the street, her heart started to chant.

The moment I said goodbye
A significant glance met my eye
I know I don't know why I know
You know maybe you unconsciously know

A wave of future nostalgic feeling surges
                    ahead of time
The Greens' friendly kindness in memory
                    flashes alive

Adieu, everybody and Nobody!
This is no "See you later, alligator"—
    "After a while, crocodile"
but, indeed, "Long Time No See"
A preconceived baby in my heart
                    enigmatically cried.

=
6
=

Yun was left alone in the grand three-story house. Her own dwelling was in the attic. She was reading *The Mad Woman in the Attic*. Her own attic was as spacious as four bedrooms, with an uneven ceiling and a few beams. It was like a watch-post. Yun sat by its small window, watching people hurrying along Wood Street. Everybody in town was busy, except her. The lazy leisure alone would turn a woman into a neurotic. She tried to resist. She was searching for company. The chirping sparrows were such low gossipers, not up to her taste. The three trees around her attic window caught her attention.

Birch

> *Bushy, boasting*
> *the peak of maturity*
> *Babbittry*
> *signifying decline*
> *a sight of gross*
> *Banality*

A Nameless Fork

> *Who are you,*
> *   Prufrock?*
> *Half-dying*
> *   Half-dangling on*
> *   the string*
> *But you do look tough*
> *   rough, the traumas*
> *   the scars, the crippled limbs*
> *   the amputated arms*
> *You are too dry to wring a tear*
> *Pinpoints of wisdom in a callous body*
> *Apathy hammered out of pathetic poetry.*

Cypress

The empress hides herself
          but I know she is there
Dashing youth—
          handsome vitality
I am longing to keep you my life
          confidant, yet
I am afraid of you, too
You are by my side
You are sneaking away.

Yun read her poems aloud, but the three trees, in the sultry evening glow, showed absolutely no response, not a stir of their leaves. Facing such a mute audience, she was unable to solo for long.

The telephone was ringing; Yun raced down the stairs. Too late. She sat there waiting. As expected, the phone rang again. It was him, the snarling-cat. He invited her to Chicago to spend the summer vacation with him. He had already arranged for an apartment for her and found her a job in a Chinese restaurant. *How did he get the phone number of my new place? How did he know that I am so lonely?* Nevertheless, it was tempting. The following day Yun went to find out the fare by Greyhound to Chicago. It was really cheap.

To go or not to go? Yun was tormented in the hot summer night. When the cooling dawn came, she decided, with a conflicted mind, not to go.

Brain massacre is over
Stagnation nursing the mind
I wonder whether I am the conqueror or the conquered
If I am a victor
          why does my heart become so numb
          utterly impossible to elicit any pleasure?
In its recess
          a cryptical voice keeps chirping:
Ha! Ha!
Still a blue-bird in a cage
          a pheasant guarded by a watchdog

> *Yes—but. . . my feeble heart*
> > *mutters with dignity*
> *This is not unwilling to escape the cage;*
> *When there's no shrine for me to beam love,*
> *A cage is better than a snare for a dove.*
> *With a self-mocking smile*
> > *the heart of the winner adds:*
> *The key to the other world is truly*
> > *in my hand.*

Yun went to her department, as it was the last day of the summer session. She met Dr. Shaw and chatted with him for a minute. After Jim left, Dr. Shaw was the advisor for graduate studies. Perhaps because he regarded it as his responsibility to take care of foreign waifs in the department, he invited Yun to visit Youngstown with his wife and son. Yun happily accepted the invitation but meanwhile felt a little guilty because of her naughtiness in his class.

╬ ╬ ╬ ╬ ╬ ╬ ╬ ╬

C Plus

"I am glad my turn comes at last. I was very sleepy and almost dozed off a minute ago. . ." Yun started her oral presentation with this statement. On the one hand the statement was true; on the other Yun intended it as a joke, to alert every listener. The whole class laughed and was fully awake. It was one of the oral presentations Yun enjoyed most. Every idea she was talking about was her own. Through Dr. Shaw's introduction, she had taken to feminist methodology. She told her audience that from a feminist point of view, Elizabeth Gaskell's *Cranford* can only be called a feminine novel. She analyzed the fables and drew a sketch of the hierarchy in that cute town of Amazons. She said "gentility" and "vulgarity" are the key words of irony. On the surface "gentility" belongs to women and "vulgarity" is a stigma of men. But ironically, "gentility" derives from gentleman and "vulgarity" associated with the vulva. Moreover, Brown, like the Party Leader in the Chinese Women's Red Detachment, is the captain while Matty, with her soft candle glow, remains a doormat in the ship of society. "Shooting Cupid" is the strength as well as the weakness of these gentrified spinsters . . . .

The whole audience seemed to be magnetized by her talk.

Tom offered her a ride home. He said, "A superb paper, Yun. I hate to hear those biographical recounts without much thought."

The following day, Lin and Hua congratulated her and said hers was the best among all the oral presentations. Yun felt flattered. But, alas, she got a C+ for the oral presentation. Worse still, hers was the lowest in the class. Even Hua, whose talk could send one easily to sleep, got an A-. Dr. Shaw soon cleared up her bewilderment: (1) You showed no respect for the other students by saying you almost dozed off when they were making their presentations; (2) by saying it was unnecessary for you to give the author's biographical information, you belittled the others who did according to my instruction; (3) your talk well passed the assigned 20 minutes. *What could I say? He was absolutely right. I was so vain and so selfish that I forgot other people's dignity and feelings. A "C" for punishment was obviously too lenient.* Still Yun was naughty. She wrote a humorous note to him:

> *Dear Professor Shaw:*
>
> *Thank you very much for giving me a "plus" for my presentation. A "plus" is a sign of ascent. Unlike a "minus," it gives one hope and encouragement.*
>
> > *Your student*
> >
> > *Yun Hu*

Actually, Yun appreciated Dr. Shaw's teaching most among the professors at Edinboro. When he played the music of Salome in class, she felt her body and soul trembling like Tuliver in *The Mill on the Floss.* She enjoyed his profound knowledge and eloquent speeches. However, Yun felt funny about having a man who had a strong interest in women's works and feminist theories remain a patriarch in class. There seemed to be some amorous feelings between Lin and Dr. Shaw. She admired him for his academic masculine traits; he liked her for her delicacy and gracefulness. Jim once said that Lin's beauty could be classified as "aristocratic." But Yun was rebellious and rustic.

━╫━ ━╫━ ━╫━ ━╫━ ━╫━ ━╫━ ━╫━ ━╫━

Yun had a wonderful day at the Youngstown mall and dined with the Shaws at the Red Lobster and Peking Garden. Everything Dr. Shaw did was proper, with style. His wife was equally considerate. She bought canned *Litchi* and a bag of fortune cookies especially for Yun. Yun was touched, and she thought of her parents at their nicer moments.

They dropped Yun off at her house. No sooner did she get in than she tore open the bag and broke a fortune cookie. The slip from the cookie said: *You will be famous and rich in your life.* Yun laughed—the Chinese always tell pleasant lies. Nevertheless, it was a sign of good luck. And good luck never travels alone. That evening Yun received a call from the English Department of University of Illinois and learned that she was being offered a teaching assistantship to complete her master's degree there. She phoned Dr. Shaw and he advised her to go as U. of I. was a much better university. But later when Yun requested a reference letter from him to support her doctoral application, he rejected her outright, because Yun left Edinboro when she had already accepted a teaching assistantship there. For this incident, Yun had enormous respect for Dr. Shaw: friendship is friendship; principle is principle. Indeed, one would rarely meet such a straight man in China, where private friendship tends to distort principles.

Once there is a place to go and a goal to strive for, one's spirit is instantly lifted up. Jogging to the Edinboro cemetery, Yun released her free spirit into the fresh air after a summer rain.

Is it wonderful to have a corner of your own
Populated with wuthering trees
and dumb tombstones

I run, I jump, I stretch my arms
Who says I am a beggar living on alms

I rub my withering skin
to breathe the wind of my second youth
I chant and dance
to the vibration of my imagination's tunes

Flippant graves whirl around me
Startled chattering birds can never appreciate thee

Bristle my heart to seek love for my self
Nobody can reach my narcissistic shelf
Monologue or soliloquy is a sign of a lunatic
Who cares since I am living in the attic

Maximum freedom is gained in a foreign void
No taboo the sound and fury of my thinking
needs to avoid.

An Ugly Duckling's Swan Song

In spite of the title
It is the other way around
Not a duckling grows into a swan
But a swan, plucking off her white feathers,
Returns to an ugly duckling
A song of debasing
The music of perversity

Drop, drop, tears of blood stitch the line
Sob, sob, quivering nose beats rhythm and rhyme
Freaks of mirth sparkle blackness of humor
Sullied heart smiles to the lotus
growing
out of the filthy silt

=
1
=

Dear Sister, you asked me how I have been getting on at Urbana-Champaign. Well, it was a nightmare, but already past, a memory almost too painful to repeat. I do not know how things have all turned against me. I am accused of plagiarism; my body has been debased; my poetic mind lost; and my brain scattered. If you really want to know the story of a neurotic, please read patiently and make the connections by yourself.

These days I have been extremely moody. One moment a nameless anger stirs up my wild spirit to an insurmountable height.

A
Wild spirit—
An impatient rocket at the end of a long countdown
Shoots to the holeless
Sky

A
Wild spirit—
A frantic spinning drill
Lets hot-blood, from the heart of the earth
Gush

A
Wild spirit—
A shriek in the wilderness
Slashes the stub of Babel to the root of Grass

A
Wild spirit—
If you are not a suicidal meteor,
you need Hurricane's eye.

Another moment I am seized by the melancholy of an unrequited lover.

I hold a cup
> *standing before the mirror*
My heart groans mutely
> *under an infinite, protean weight*

Black bile oozing, tickling
along my rugged blood funnels
from the tips of my fingers
dripping into the cup

My chapped lips command:
> *Please laugh or aloud you cry!*
My ears crane their necks but cannot hear
My eyes, whipping their lashes, still cannot see
My hi-fi nerves fail to feel:

Who can make me laugh or cry—I
will give him a mountain of gold!
Ethereal mountains of gold, silver, and diamond
echo, mock, and guffaw
for no gods dare to claim my reward

My lips kiss the bitter mouth of the cup
> *suck all the poison of melancholy*
> > *and smash the cup disdainfully:*

If you cannot laugh or cry
> *die!*
> > *die!*
> > > *die!*

Do you remember about half a year ago when you received my first letter from University of of Illinois, you wrote back: "You the little ugly duckling has finally grown into a swan." I thought so, too. I started writing little English poems when I was in Edinboro. One could hardly call my scratches poems, as they are all written in a rough, spontaneous manner. You know I never showed interest in poetry when I was in China.

I happened to take a course in British Romanticism last semester. Perhaps writing little poems already had loosened me to flippancy. I was enchanted by the professor of that course. His voice was musical, his young appearance led me to take him as the incarnation of Byron or Shelley.   He finally became my muse and led me to write the long poem, "Oh, Oh, Oh—A Romantic Parody." You begged me many times to send you that poem. I was too shy then to send it. Now I have turned so ugly that I no longer mind anybody probing my heart with a scalpel.

1

Oh, Orlando
What are you to me?
My eyes delight at the presence of Adam
My ears enjoy the sweetest melody
A spring bee sporting in the wind
                              to seduce the belated peony to bloom
Only makes me feel withering
                   like the tassels of a broom
My marital filaments
                   floating in the air
Who knows who
                   will notice and care
I do not mind whether you're free or bound
Though I do see other flowers lurking
                   in the background
I may have power to hypnotize
But no power to create
                   a romance in paradise
Never dare to dream a night in heaven
Only cherish the moments when we happened
Sit side by side, so close—
I could hear the synchronous beating
                   of our hungry drums
Then, the moments in my memory
                   double
                              triple
                                        multiply
To fill the pauses of brooding
                   in my life
Is this the convergence of subconscious and
                              conscious love?
Is this of the first and last, and midst and without end?

2

Oh, Dryle
What a strange name to me!
I sailed over the sea of dictionaries and
            drained all the fresh water of my brain tank
Could only arrive at the port of "Delai'er"
I know what this signifies—
It can never be assimilated into Chinese
As my name "Yun"
Can never be submerged into English
Without hiccups and pain
Yet still
        I wish
                I wish
                        I wish
I wish my wish could be fulfilled for one wink
Then I would die
I would turn into an ash butterfly
Like the meanest flower guarding the tomb
Watching a bat hovering over the
                        dome of doom.

3

Oh, you are a Tyger
        I am a Tyger, too
I presage we'll fight each other
You believe we can become one—
            then must be a fearful symmetry:
The marriage of Tygerness and Lambness
            between Heaven and Hell
(Are you scared? Maybe
Maybe, it's not too late to escape:
Let one stay in the jungle of the light
The other hide in the forests of the night).

This poem has the camouflage of William Blake's "The Tyger" and Virginia Woolf's *Orlando*. The androgynous Orlando (that professor) and I are both 36. We must have been coincidentally born in the year of the tiger. You remember that I was born not only in the year of the tiger but in the month of Leo, don't you?

    After I wrote the poem, I drew a red flower on a stem crossing the ashen body of a strange creature resembling a dragonfly.

> *What is it?!*
> *A peony or a rose?*
> *A butterfly or a bat?*
> *The eyes are those of a tiger*
> *The antennae are phoenix feathers*
> *The body is that of a dragonfly*
> *The stem is a broomstick*
> *It echoes*
> *It emanates*
> *It is beaten black and blue*
> *It bleeds*
> *Every part of it blurs into the crying vortex*
> > *while you are zipping your eyes*
> > > *collages into a beatific union*
> > *when you open your vision.*

=
2
=

Dear Sister, you suspected that I had fallen in love with my professor. Perhaps I did. But it was on a different level—he was my idol of Romanticism and my muse. As if he had given me a magic wand, no matter what I touched with the wand, it became a poem. When I saw the bald pine tree in our desolate back garden, poetic lines threaded out like from a silkworm:

Winter is encroaching
      upon the self-abandoning garden
Flowers flip their petals to touch the final dews
Trees squander away their color
      to beg passersby's last glimpse of beauty
There, Bald Pine stands in solemnity
      with noises of Babel puffing from inside:

Many bygone silvery winters
      envied my perennial green
      and happy birds nestled in my crotches
Now, pheasants have flown away
Butterflies no longer flutter around my knees
Even squirrels are seeking new playgrounds. . .
Foggy rains lash my withered bark
      tearing sinews of my heart
A flash of glow-bugs makes me duck my head
Suddenly I've found the vines of Morning Glory
      creeping around me
Her tiny palms are tenderly green
Her tulips are white and pink
She has twined around my trunk
            like a serpent
In full bloom she
            hymns to the bellows of my aging lungs:

My dear Baby
Don't be forlorn
Riding on the emerald wings

Breaths of love push you along
Lotus petals flank your hollow trunk
Fingers of Muse pluck up a passionate song
At Christmas
        you won't feel alone
My blushing bells will jingle, jingle
                all night long.

I scribbled one or two poems every day. My poetic aspiration was by no means confined to the theme of love. For instance, one day when I watched it drizzle from a window in my office at the English Building, I seemed to see the scene of a storm I watched there the other day.

Watching a Storm

A violent downfall
Yet I see no cats and dogs
On one eave of a low building
        hanging a tuft of beautifully permed hair
                of a wild tornado
The shining, flat, supple bodies of bespectacled cobras
    undulating hurriedly on the drifting ripples
            of the grassy icicles
                    along the concrete roads
From all directions
                towards one direction
Like icebergs of raging wheels
        floating to Tian An Men Square
            on that April morning

The orgy of thunder and lightning
        carelessly reveals
                the subtle shades of autumn colors
Premature apricot yellow
Adolescent orange orange
An elusive serious dark blue of the ancient political animal
The nude redness of a wet, meaty lip in its prime
I have often thought
        (but who has put it so well
            so perceptive and worldly wise):
No money can buy the colors in a storm

I prefer downpour to drizzling
Drizzling, a mere misty veil
Downpour, a sauna of purgation
A vapor of howling rampage
         ushers in
                  a softer and fresher Apollo.

I believe you will like this poem. That April morning in 1976, you were beaten by a policeman and your brother was stuffed into a gunnysack and dragged to prison. I wish I could have scratched a poetic line on Tian An Men Square. But even if I could write poems, being a gullible fool then, I would not have climbed on a freight train to Beijing like you.

Perhaps you are tired of reading my poems by now. Please, take your time. Read them slowly, better one or two a day or a week. I must send you the seven-section poem called "A Fashion Show." I received enthusiastic applause after I read it at the poetry club.

1

My clothes were aged with premature wrinkles.
I did not comb my night-ruffled hair.
My face, naked, dims and glows as it is.

"Good morning, Miss Hu!" A human
Voice greeted me.

Startled by a singing rooster at dawn,
I put on my best dress with feminine delicacy,
After Nipples puffed to ripe mulberries in the shower,
Fingers of carrots meddled with Hair half an hour,
Magnified Eyes, contoured Lips, and
tapered Nails stole an hour and a half.

"Good morning, Miss Hu." A human
Voice still recognized me.

2

I tightened my glistening belt,
put on the brightest color,
imitated the perfect carriage,
held the composure of my gender.

"Miss Hu, you look so sad."

I did not know what I was wearing—
a carefree body in a careless float,
passing like wind driving fallen leaves.

"Miss Hu, you do look smart!"

3

Necklace is chain
Earrings are hooks
Bras and tights
        bandages and coats of mails
They crystallize Snow White in a glass coffin
Deep freeze a tender shoot of an antique bamboo
                in early spring

You're so lucky to be a woman
        privileged
                to enjoy the shimmering of the world
                        without embarrassment
You're so lucky to be a woman
                to indulge in self-affliction
                        without any resentment.

4

I used to dress for outsiders
Saving the best for sightseeing
I used to dress for my secretly chosen fiance
Groping this or that way to fathom his inscrutable taste

Now I dress up for nobody
but myself

A serene night
I put on my best
Standing before a life-long mirror
Turn on the rambling music
Languidly move my floating limbs like
a fairy of starfish
Dart here and there
an inebriated poet
Spilling nectar out of a celestial boat

A hundred princes are
vying to kiss my shadow
A thousand emperors are
gilding themselves at
the dusty aureole of my big toe

I, like Daiyu, in a
Dream of the Red Chamber[1]
Listlessly flip my ample sleeves
like a coin
Let all male flowers flee
like flies
twirl
like ballerinas of frost
in a musical gust
of the romantic wind

The beatific ecstasy
knocks me into a swoon
Hugging the fluffy white rabbit
of the solitary moon[2]
With a heart-expanding smile
in my best look

---

[1] Daiyu, a delicate and aloof female rebel in the *Dream of the Red Chamber*, is known for burying flowers while a Chinese fairy is known for scattering flowers in the air. Here is a parodic fusion of Daiyu's spirit and the fairy's deed.

[2] According to Chinese myth, Chang E swallowed elixir stolen from her husband and flew to the moon, only to suffer solitude, for there is no one else but a rabbit on the moon.

Murmuring hypnotically:
Oh, I feel so good
so good
so good. . . .

5

I love clothes
I buy the fashionable thing
I use makeup
I wear necklace and ring
Off the dressing table
everything but me
retreats to oblivion
I dive into my professional obsession
like a loon
Forget all, but turn into a well-ornamented
Dynamo
puffing irresistible power.

6

See how natural and careless I look
Who knows I've worked on it for three hours

Then my sartorial care never stops
I constantly caress every ripple to
make it more careless and natural

The genuine geranium, the man-made rose
Who can tell
which is artificial?
which is real?

A baboon is so natural as to
dangle her prime femaleness
between her legs
Only to turn true seers away.

7

At a dazzling party
Every body is painfully dressed
Men in suits and ties
Women on high heels
> *emitting halos of gold*
I surpass them all
> *with an intruder's*
> > *shabby coat*

In a routine day
People forget to polish their leathers
> *ignoring how they look*
Everybody is shrouded with a shred
> *of one overall*
I put on my best suit
> *parading through them*
> > *like a blooming atom bomb*

Plain as the plains
Humble like a ravine
Higher than Everest
Fashion kills the fashion wind.

Sister, each model in this fashion show represents a fracture of the multifarious me. The way a person dresses reveals her personality, but not always. You know I have a style of my own. Even during those bleak days of the Cultural Revolution I liked to dress differently from others. Do you still remember Old Zhao said that his impression of me was as a girl in blue pants with two faded patches on the knees and one on the hips. I did not know patched pants could be very fashionable until I came to America. If you think feminists do not care about what they wear, you are 50% wrong. Some of them do care a lot. Daring to dress is a feminist statement. However, taste is of vital importance. When I see some Chinese ladies dress gaudily, I can smell the emptiness of their minds. I am glad that the Chinese aesthetic taste has been individualized lately.

=
3
=

Sister, excuse me for my digression. What was I talking about? Pain.   Writing to you is such a relief that I almost forget my pain.

Right, I fell in love with my professor, purely because he was to me the image of Romanticism.   I never associated him with any ordinary sense of love.   When I thought of him, I felt uplift-ed and poetic.   He obviously appreciated my sensitivity.   When I got back my paper on Shelley's "Ozymandias" with the request, "May I have a photocopy of this essay, please?", I felt thrilled, as though I had received a love letter.   He liked all my interpreta-tions of poems, except the one on the celebration of female beauty in Keats' "To Autumn."   It was an intentional misreading of Keats' poem;   nevertheless, my interpretation fits into almost every image and every line perfectly.   You know our Chinese way of reading poems.   During the Cultural Revolution, every-body read themselves or their own situations into Mao Zedong's poems or poetic catchwords.   That was how we made his poetry known from door to door.   Even today we quote Tang lines or Song phrases for spring couplets to paste on the doors and gates. Do we ever care much what their authors originally meant? What we care about is how an ancient line can still convey the new meaning of today.   Undoubtedly, the theories of Stanley Fish were far behind the Chinese readers' practices.   I was aware of our bad habit of raping a poem to produce a child of our own, but I did not wish to yield to my professor, as he seemed to be trying hard to subdue me.

Still autumn for the master,
Already winter for the pupil.

Please don't be so kind as to be cruel!
Can I type it after your approval?

Half an hour for you, an hour and a half for me.
Three papers to be written and typed this climatic week.
The headlong denouement is crushing on my fading smile.

A matter of survival?

Time, Time, please become an elastic string.
Fractured Grecian Urn, Earthen Pot, please turn into
a barbed wire in a bush,
To trip the trumping feet of the Clock.

To love is to be subdued.
To fight is to be a loser.
To be a student is to be minced/geared in/to the iron-faced
academic Machine.

Reading the above unpoetic verse, you will see how hard it is to be a graduate student in America if English is not your mother tongue and you do not even type it well. But I managed to get through every paper in time. With a deep sigh of relief, I started to address Christmas cards for the professors who had taught me that semester. I loved them all and each of them had fed me with magnanimity.

Anu came in, a beautiful Indian girl, with long glossy dark hair and eyes of wisdom. Seeing I was busy with Christmas cards, she said:

"I used to do that in my first year but I outgrew it a long time ago. People here do not give a dime to human care. Why bother doing it?"

Compared with this Indian girl, I was aged but still innocent as a baby about human relationships.

"You like Dr. Dryle, do you? He is okay, but not that handsome. Perhaps you have not heard that he is gay. "

"Gay? What does gay mean?"

"Homosexual. Everybody else in the department knows. He and Dr. Marlowe are lovers."

"Really? Marlowe, that old man?" On the verge of saying that ugly, old man, I swallowed the "ugly. "

"Yes. That old man is a fox. Be watchful."

That girl, like an angel sent by God, after revealing the truth, left me in the cold.

I suddenly felt my whole existence was threatened. Dryle and Marlowe, it is impossible. Yes, possible. It must be true. My brain was racing fast. I remembered during our last talk, Marlowe said, "Professor Dryle often praises you for your poetic talent. He likes your poetry. Why don't you take him as your

lover and write some love poems?" Dear me, I did not know then
he was jealous, he was warning me, he was giving me signals.
What shall I do? Dryle is my thesis advisor and Marlowe the
director for graduate students.

I was paralyzed in the office for two hours. When I got home,
I asked Edward, the host of the house, how a man can be homosexual. He took my question rather lightly.

"Not only a man, but a woman can also be homosexual.
Don't tell me you haven't noticed Margaret and Ruth are lesbians?"

Just then Margaret and Ruth came in. Edward called to
them:

"Hey, tell Yun. Aren't you lesbians?"

The two women, one in pants and the other in a miniskirt,
said earnestly, "Yeah, we two have been living together since
last year." Ruth hugged Margaret.

I did not know what to say. When I said I was shocked to
hear that two of my professors were gay, Edward said, "Not
merely two. I know the Director of Computer Science is also
gay. In fact this place is known as Little Berkeley. Perhaps
one-third of the people on campus are homos. I can show you
their nightclub, if you want."

I was dumbfounded by such a revelation of daffodils,
"Besides the lake, beneath the trees, / Fluttering and dancing in
the breeze." I excused myself by saying that I had a headache
and went to bed.

I wept that night, my heart broken. It was the first time that I
realized I loved Dryle so personally that I could not tolerate reality.

Blake's sooty waif weeps, weeps
   in drippings of cold,
To Keats's choir of the mourning gnats
      and treble soft singing of the crickets;

The red-breast whistles in a cursing world
Where the twilight of Autumn winds up
Before the morning glow of Spring fades out;

An unfledged swallow twitters in the air,
Asking Shelley with audacity of love:
Should she warm her body under the eaves
Or frost her head in the West Wind?

For one moment I thought of Oscar Wilde and Lord Byron and tried to convince myself that true artists are gay because they love beauty in themselves too much. Dryle must be inno- cent. Dryle is Billy Budd and he is seduced by that ugly Claggart Marlowe, who clawed upon him like a serpent twisting around a young sapling. At another moment I felt Dryle had de- ceived me with his innocent front. He was the sinner of an un- pardonable crime. I was tired and my brain lost its waking function. I had a nightmare in which I saw Dryle, with old shoes hanging from his neck, being paraded through my farm and a crowd was chasing after him with scissors. I woke up in agony. This had happened in 1979 when I was on a Youth Farm. One day my classmate Mali was paraded, with his hair scis- sored like a madman. He had allegedly attempted to rape his roommate Tieming. How could a male ever rape a male? But it was happening. I had seen Court announcements about men sentenced to death for taking liberties with young boys and men put in jail for the crime of "Jijian"—"raping a rooster." This had been a mystery to me until I saw a German movie. God per- haps never expected the human anus to be upgraded for sex. I did not know why Dryle had had broken shoes around his neck in my dream. This is normally reserved for the parading of a whore.

The following day Edward took me to the mall to buy Christmas gifts. I moved along with him like a robot. I could not get over Dryle, my idol of Romanticism. That night I wept so much that my tears composed a Christmas gift.

My Christmas Gift—
A Pair of Tearful Eyes

In this gift-giving season,
Pain-philter dissolves my body into acid water
                              within a dead bay.
Nothing left but a pair of tearful eyes.
I want to offer them to some-body with the embers of my love;
But no-body wants them at such a merry-making time:
Can they decorate the Christmas Tree?

The betrayed eyes swell into a pavilion
In the middle of a stagnant lagoon;
Tears drip from its uplifted eaves,

Pattering rhythmically on withered lotus leaves.

The rejected eyes spring into a twin-tower on the tip of a cliff.
Torrents of tears, from one canopy tumbling
                              over the nose bridge,
Eagerly merging into the corrugated reservoir of the other,
Gathering at the tilted antique dragon jaws,
Unsluice their pearly cascade into the heartless pillow ravine.

The abandoned eyes hover like two trunkless leaves,
Searching for the happy, happy bough of the heaven.
Ah, sweetness in acerbity is sweeter,
Is bitterness in honey the bitterest?
Bitterness is truth, truth bitter.
This is all I know, and nobody else needs to know.

The eyes are my poetic self. I felt wretched for the destruction of my muse. It was not he but I who was betrayed and abandoned.

=
4
=

Dear Sister, if you think disillusionment would save a lost soul and reality would teach me some cool rationality, you are wrong. I was totally weighed down by pain. I wept day and night and my mind would not take in one word of my forced reading. I was trying to drill into Wordsworth's "The Ruined Cottage," which was selected as a major poem for my master's thesis, but all I got was a vision of my body expanding and collapsing into that ruined cottage.

To shake off the vision, I took a walk into the woods behind the campus. That was the day before Christmas Eve and nobody had time to view the bleak nature detached from their fireplace.

A lake girdled by a tar belt.
Trees sheathed by dead vines.
Humidity holds the Nightingale by her throat.
Woodpecker, for whom do you knock the death knell?
Teeming head weighs down the jogging feet
Dragging along no flesh and bones but a ton of rotten meat.
A gray fish wags its tail in a ditch.
"I am not you, who knows you do not enjoy a fill of melancholy.
Since you fall in love with drab water,
Be content with your tamed fins.
Why do your dorsal eyes still look at my wild wings?"

A red serpent with black golden rings tempts
Billy Budd with the apple of her wisdom eye.
If Billy has never opened his innocent mouth,
how could the apple slip into his throat?
Laggard, droning his envy for beauty,
blows liquid of ugliness into the ear of the unbloomed Budd.
Queen-moon sees this and changes the shape of her face,
turning into a silver-ringed dark cloud.
With an angry cry, she swoops down upon the earth,
Unhapply only to smack the lips of the lightning rod.
Meteors pour down from her milliard eyes,

All in vain, only stirring dust from the mirror of the lake.
There is no sympathy or pity for you to fish.
The coiled serpent, rolling in the apple of her eye,
breathes virus from its darting fang,
playing an incantation on the Aeolian harp:
Never be hanged into heaven
But perish by the single-sexed love-sin.

Self-righteousness gave me momentary feelings of anger and hatred. Love allures, often making one lose one's head whereas anger and hatred pump up strength. Anger and hatred are not the hotbed of frustration. Frustration belongs to the coward.

Something in my life I never wanted to know—the truth of reality.

Damned Anu, why did you tell me the truth when I was not ready to face the sun?

Oh, poetry, you have become my enemy. You poisoned me, almost murdered me. You are so repulsive. I shall never. . . .

But dear Sister, you must be aware of my self dramatizing. You know malice is not really in my nature. The truth is I love him, especially at a wrong age and in a wrong place. Although our culture has taught me that love is the detonator—once lighted, you destroy and you are self-destroyed—my love for him refuses to be killed. It seems to be infinite; when I die, it will haunt me in my afterlife.

When I dragged myself home, Edward told me our neighbor needed a babysitter overnight for their two kids because she was going to a party with her boyfriend. I agreed. Doing something perhaps could free me from my crazy obsession.

After the kids went to bed, I sat alone by the telephone table thinking. I could hear the splitting of my nerves, exactly like a horrible scene in a movie—numerous fragmented thoughts, images, shouts attacking me from all directions at once. I was going mad. The last nerve of rationality in my hand dialed a number—I was not conscious of whose.

"Hello, is it Yun?" Luckily, it was Edward.

I burst out crying.

"I am coming over."

It was already past midnight. When Edward came to me, I grabbed him like a mad woman. We tumbled to the floor. He did not say anything, but kissed me, caressed me, and invaded my body that had abstained from sex during the past twenty months.

After Edward left, I had a long, long sleep until the kids woke me up at eleven in the morning. I quickly cooked some pancakes for them and tidied the house up. Their single parent came home, looking tired but still happy.

I went home and saw Edward smiling. He looked gentle and affectionate, saying he was going to buy a dishwasher so that I did not need to wash dishes a couple of times a day. He was cleaning the house himself and his kids were tidying up their own rooms. Edward had never said a word of seduction to me; I never felt sexually threatened in his house. But my body had been profaned by him. The profaning of the body stopped my symptoms of madness. I really do not know how to make out all these funny incidents. I did not loathe Edward; instead I felt sorry for him—I had borrowed his body to keep myself from falling apart.

Edward cooked a wonderful Christmas dinner. Everybody was in a cheerful mood. I looked placid, my mind was degrading in the lull of an aftermath, too dumb to recall a past nightmare. After all the kids fell asleep, Edward tiptoed to my room. He lay down by my side and asked me what was torturing me. I told him of my love for Dr. Dryle as the idol of Romantic poetry and how I could not cope with his destruction.

"Dryle? A friend of mine knows him. I heard he used to be a priest."

"A priest? How could a priest be gay?"

"A priest is also a human being."

Edward wanted to make love and I refused.

"When you need to masturbate, please let me help you." Edward left.

I lay awake for almost the whole night, rethinking the relationship between Dr. Dryle and Dr. Marlowe. Extramarital sex is a sin. Since I was a sinner now, the ugly reality became more acceptable. I had been thinking too much. I felt dizzy, as if my bed was sinking into the earth. All colors and all boundaries blurred. The dawn was arriving. The shadows of dancing flakes outside the window led me to musing.

**For
Musing
On Christmas**

*White, white Edelweiss
Red, red Rose
Is Edelweiss really white? Is Rose really red?
Can a rose be white?   Can an edelweiss
be red?
Is Edelweiss ever flamed? How often is rose chilled?
Is
Edelweiss always white?   Does Rose have to
be sullied?
Snow-adorned Edelweiss   Red-sullied Rose
Folks!
At the white Christmas
Let our frosted lips touch
the redwine distilled from the
sullied roses.*
**Ch
ee
rs!
Queen-Moon**

Merry Christmas!

=
5
=

Dear Sister, you are right. By the beginning of the spring semester, I had mostly overcome my cultural shock or psychological hangups, ready to reconcile with Dr. Dryle and Dr. Marlowe. Quite unexpectedly, I got my grade report and discovered a C for a course on pedagogy. I thought it was a recording mistake, as I had received an A- for one major paper and B+ for another. But I found out that there had not been a mistake. The C was due to the fact that I did not do what the course had required for a little paper (instead of listing reference books guiding a reader to a bibliography on George Eliot, I compiled a selected bibliography). This is the second C in my life (not even a plus this time) and the only C for a course. I was upset and thought it necessary to let Dr. Dryle know as he was my thesis advisor. Well, I was ironically tricked by my own trust. When Dr. Dryle saw my little paper for that course, he said that a C was too high because I had plagiarized a portion of a bibliography from a book every professor knew.

I was puzzled. How could one plagiarize a bibliography? Is it like plagiarizing a dictionary?

Being Chinese, I never regarded plagiarism as a serious crime though I was aware of how Americans felt about it. When I was sitting at the writing center, I heard people talking about Kim, a graduate student from Korea, who had just been just expelled from the department because his essay had some plagiarized phrases and sentences. I remembered Liu told me Wang transferred himself from English to economics because Dr. Marlowe caught him plagiarizing. Now nearly every university knows the problem with Chinese students in America. If a professor is really strict, he or she can easily find a way to flunk a Chinese. I had heard all of this but never believed that I was committing plagiarism. Thinking hard, I remembered that day when I borrowed numerous books on George Eliot from the library; I had skillfully flipped to the back of each book and typed the items I wanted on the computer. I did not even check the authors or titles of those books. Still I could not accept the accusation of being a plagiarist.

I went to Dr. Walden and asked him whether he gave me a C because I had plagiarized. He absolutely refused to make an accusation in that direction. He insisted that he had given me a C simply because I had not written what he had assigned. Perhaps he was too kind to kill a Chinese graduate with that accusation. Plagiarism is too severe a crime for anyone to survive in the academic world. Not only the academic world—when I got home that day, Edward happened to laugh at the stupidity of a man running for president. Can you imagine how stupid he is? In his campaign speech he plagiarized the inauguration speech of a former president. Who? What has he plagiarized? How can he plagiarize since every word is known to the nation and his speech is open to the public? That is exactly how he tried to defend himself. Read the paper, listen to the radio, the whole nation is talking about his plagiarism. I did not want to read the news or listen to the radio. I did not want to know who he was. If a statement was good for the nation in the past why could he not use it again? Doesn't history often repeat itself?

I felt I was wronged by the intellectual private ownership of a capitalist world. I had no tears and my eyes were dry like sand. That night I had a funny dream.

An extra-terrestrial came to me and led me to a balloon-like room. Instructed by brain waves, I put on a pair of magic shoes and shrouded myself with a cellophane veil. Pressing a button, I traveled in the universe with the alien. Chinese ancestors believed angels could travel by stepping on two clouds. If they lived today, they would see that science has enabled men to pass angels at last. The veil sealed me into a cocoon. It must have been insulated as I could see the stars and moon and everything zooming by but felt neither cold nor lack of oxygen. I felt comfortable as if lying on a sofa in the sitting room. The brain waves told me I could switch the light on and read a book if I was hungry.

I was amused. But pretty soon, the alien guided me to his planet. It was an inquisitive world indeed. As soon as I arrived, numerous extra-terrestrials asked about our world. I told them the urgent problem for our planet was overpopulation.

"That! We solved it about two thousand years ago. Do you feel our world is crowded?"

No. Their streets were wide, flanked with flowers and trees. From one house to another there was at least an acre of space. And there were no skyscrapers. Most of the buildings were shaped like balloons or torpedoes.

"Put on this astroscope."

"Wow." I saw so many balloons and torpedoes floating on the water like paramecia, layer after layer, paving a ladder to the ninth heaven.

"Since we designed these houses that can float or anchor anywhere in the sky like ships on the sea, people can have as many children as they like. Of course, there is order, like navigation routes on your high seas. Due to vibrations, those houses will never crash into one another. Have you seen one fish run into another in the water?"

"The higher you live, the thinner the air. How do you breathe?"

"Breathe? Nobody does that primitive act any more. When a baby is born here, he or she is given a lump of concentrated oxygen, enough to last 120 years."

"What do you eat then?"

" We eat words."

I remembered that the brain waves had instructed me to read a book if I felt hungry.

" Words? Do you still have problems such as indigestion, constipation, and heartburn?"

" Yes. If you eat the words you do not understand, or you are word-gluttonous, or eat only certain words, you will have personal problems."

"Personal problems? Does anyone in your world have a problem with plagiarism?"

"That is not a problem. We take plagiarism as the highest virtue. Look!"

I looked in the direction he was pointing to and saw a large crowd of people standing in a place like Times Square. When my guide took me there, I saw two huge slogans hanging on the stage: (1) All books under heaven are due to plagiarism; and (2) Plagiarism is beauty. All the aliens were having a friendly contest to see who could be elected the King or Queen of Plagiarism for the year. The judges, I was told, were the most studious bookworms of the country. They had to know all the famous classics as well as gutter literature to identify the original sources of a word, phrase, or quote. It was a tough job, I guess. I could only identify the first slogan, which was stolen from my father, but I failed to identify the other.

Perhaps I had stared at the slogan for too long and I had the overwhelming urge to go to the bathroom.

"Where is the ladies' room?"

"The public bathroom is over there. We do not separate ladies from gentlemen in things like producing excrement."

I went there and saw piles of papers. A warning sign said: ONE BOOK AT A TIME. And an eye-catching slogan with the words "One person's excrement is another's food" was hanging on the front wall. *I see, defecating for them is producing books like ours.* Fortunately, my stomach felt okay again.

I came out, resuming my questions.

"Since you do not eat food like earthlings, what do you do every day?"

"Creativity. Producing books. Nobody even bothers to go to the bathroom any more. The only power is the brain—thinking. Have you noticed that everybody in our world wears a little device on the wrist?"

"Yes, a wristwatch. Very common on our Earth."

"No. We do not need watches. Our people do not have any concept of time. What everyone is wearing is a brain-video which shows whatever you are thinking—in fact, thinking is never in words alone but is always accompanied by images, emotions, and dialogues. Books or written words can never capture the real thinking accurately. We finally solved this problem. One can revise one's own thinking by pushing a relay knob here. The device can record and retrieve whatever you feel you would like to share with another person, like a book. However, according to our statistics in recent years, people are getting too narcissistic, only reviewing their own thoughts. That is why we have learned something from China in your world and hold plagiarism as an incentive for people to read and use others' ideas."

"But I haven't seen any books around."

"Oh, you mean the books from your Earth. The books from other planets have all been recorded onto minitapes and transmitted through brain waves. They are available from sunrise to moonset. Come and put on this brain-video. Have you started reading? Do you hear the sound effects, taste the succulent flavors, sweet, sour, bitter, salty. . . . I see you enjoy munching apples, chewing gum. Don't be too greedy, or you'll be satiated soon. Be careful, or you will become overweight. . . ."

The alarm clock rang. My saliva wet the pillow.

The dream made me feel better. But when I saw Dr. Dryle about my draft on the images of women in Romantic poetry, I was thrown into an abyss. He had asked me to show him all of the reference books I had borrowed for my project and then compared them with my writing. After doing so, he found I had mixed my own thoughts with others' criticism. He was very angry and ordered me to stop my project and change to a new topic. For this new topic, I was forbidden to read even one book of criticism.

Only one and a half months remained before the deadline for my master's thesis, but I had to start anew. I remembered a story I had heard in Edinboro. A graduate student near the completion of his dissertation was ordered by his Chair to change to a new topic. He could no longer finish his dissertation. Before he died, he said he would haunt that Chair when he became a ghost. Perhaps he could never become a ghost, because no professor could ever be haunted by a student.

Although I felt the merciless edge of a tyrannical sword, I had actually received a big favor—no more research, no more plagiarism. I chose Wordsworth's long poem "Michael" as my new project. I read "Michael" forward, backward, vertically, horizontally, and diagonally. I named my thesis "Three Visions of Michael: Archetype, Individualist, Poet." With Michael's unconquerable spirit, I wrote furiously and finished surprisingly fast. Dr. Dryle crossed out the lines about my association with the Enclosure Movement in England on the grounds that I could not have known this without a secondary source. You know, Chinese children learn about it in primary school. Never mind. I completed my MA by the end of April.

=
6
=

Dear Sister, I left out a good many of the ugly things that happened during those nightmarish four months. I surrendered my body to Edward again and again. There was a perversity in me that led to a deliberate demoralization. I never cared what Edward was thinking about me. When we were having sex, I merely treated him as a clinical instrument. Nevertheless, there was a visible change in Edward. He started writing poems about daisies and crab apples. One day, he gave me a film ticket and said the ticket had been given to him by one of his colleagues. I suspected he had bought it especially for me. I enjoyed that comedy enormously. It was called "The Gods Must Be Crazy." On my birthday he bought me a rosebud. I did not even put it in a vase. It soon died of thirst. Naturally, I could feel Edward's resentment toward me.

He started reaching out to all sorts of women. Poor Edward was busying himself with making appointments, inviting people for dinner, and looking for romance. He changed women like a model changing outfits. There was no end to his new, short-lived lovers. It was hard for me to detest him. He told me that his love was fragmented and he liked all sorts of women. He must cling to women to disperse his restlessness and uncertainty about human feelings and even life. He tried to offer his harmless body (he had a vasectomy after his third child and did not have any sexually transmitted diseases) to as many women as possible. Young girls, single women, separated, divorced, or unhappy wives all need him in their distress. He told me that any woman who had made love with him once could turn to him at any time, even his ex-wife. I could see why women loved him like Baoyu in *The Dream of the Red Chamber*.

I remembered that at the last grand party for Edward's birthday all of his lovers or would-be lovers came. An elegant and intelligent-looking lady, who had two master's degrees and was pursuing her PhD in philosophy, came to my room and asked, "Who is that gross woman Edward embraced a moment ago?"

"Peggy, I guess. She was his girlfriend when I first came."

The elegant woman was tortured. She told me how Edward had caught her eye the other day and she had such a passion for him, but he seemed to have ignored her. It was true that Edward loved intellectual women but he felt more comfortable with "gross" women like Peggy. Edward was a down-to-earth man and never pretended he was not.

Edward also had his spiritual side. I remember that on Easter, he had woken at three o'clock in the morning to watch the sunrise over the lake. He was not very lucky that year. It was chilly at the beach. He made a fire and waited patiently. When dawn finally came, he first saw a crow (a bad omen in Chinese) and then a beaver (a hard-working type) at sunrise. The following day he stayed overnight with Lucy and came back with a little kerosene lamp. He said he was with Lucy the whole night, talking about romance. *Did you make love with her? No, she did not want to and gave me this lamp to remember her by.* Whenever he talked about his latest girlfriend, Edward would adopt the tone of Ah Q.[3] " Well, great progress, but not ready yet. It takes some time to warm up." I would say, "Prince Charming, you have to take some initiative. Don't be too shy. "

He had a trusting nature and confided to me almost everything about his private life. He said his wife had divorced him because he had had an affair with their babysitter.

"After your divorce, why didn't you marry that babysitter?"

"Don't you know Pamela? She was our babysitter. She looked beautiful with her long hair then." Pamela later cropped her hair like a boy and turned lesbian.

I remembered that whenever Pamela would come to the house, she would pounce on Edward like a long-time-no-see lover. They would become tangled together, playing like a puppy and a cat. Pamela said many times that she loved Edward and he was the best man in the world.

"Then, why did you turn lesbian?"

" Well, after having sexual experiences with many men, I found myself truly enjoying relationships with women. Perhaps it is a family tradition or a biological thing. My brother is also homosexual."

I was finally recovered from my cultural shock caused by homophobia. I also came to accept my fate to be punished as the scapegoat of China's plagiarism. Do you remember the funny discovery I told you about during our study in Shanghai in 1983?

---

[3] Ah Q, a character created by Lu Xun, is famous for turning his defeat into a psychological victory.

I told you that I had read nine articles on American black humor and found seven of them expressed the same thoughts and three of them have paragraphs in the exact same wording. It was impossible for me to find out who was the original writer until I came to America. The Chinese habitually committed plagiarism largely because of their conceptual lack of individualism—this lack is perhaps a birthmark of socialism. Since 1978, China has obviously grasped some Western capitalist straws for revitalization, yet it repacked those straws with the label of "Socialism With China's Unique Features." Confucius says, "If the name is not right; the words will be crooked." Having benefited from plagiarism, China seems to have become a mule—neither horse nor donkey.

Dr. Marlowe had been sick this semester. Sometimes, Dr. Dryle would say, "Sorry I could not finish reading your draft in time. This weekend I had to take care of Dr. Marlowe in the hospital." I remembered once while I was talking about the love and tolerance of a mother, Dr. Dryle snorted suspiciously. His mother must not have loved him. Perhaps his father was a loving being. He clung to Dr. Marlowe like a son to a father. He had been merciless to me; apart from enforcing righteous academic principles, he must have felt that my "problem" and my "plagiarism" were endangering his career. He wished to remove me as quickly as possible. But behind his cruel mask were the vulnerability and insecurity of a child. Although I was becoming a wreck, I had sympathy and cared for him.

One day I had lunch with Alex, a poet residing on campus. His office was located next to Dr. Dryle's.

"I heard him shouting at you. What's the matter? You should report his behavior to the department."

I shed tears. "No, nothing. I have been a mother. I have no roots here. Once I am gone I am gone. But this will perhaps be his academic homeland for life."

"I have served in the army and done all sorts of odd jobs. I do not trust those who go from school to school all their lives. They simply do not know much about life. I mean, they do not understand humanity. Hard to grow up just in books. . . ."

During my last talk with the department, the Chair asked, "Why did your choose him as your advisor?"

"He offered."

"Why didn't you change to another professor when you had problems with him?"

"Changing horses in midstream could have been worse. I

am going away but he has to stay. I must say that he has done nothing wrong in advising me. He is extremely responsible. No matter how busy he is, he has read every draft carefully. Without his help, it would have been impossible for me to complete the thesis in such a short time."

I did not know whether there were rumors about me in the department. I had never breathed my trouble to anybody. By the end of that semester, a graduate student asked me whether she should put Dr. Dryle on her doctoral committee.

"By all means do it. He is a responsible advisor. And his expertise will help you with your work."

"But my brother advised me not to. He said he is an odd person, a gay."

"I don't know about that. He seems to me a very sincere, disciplined scholar. Anyway, his personal lifestyle has nothing to do with your dissertation, has it?"

On the last day of the semester, I packed my things, ready to leave the English Building once and for all. Surprisingly I saw that old, shriveled Dr. Marlowe standing in the sunlight, smiling at me. He was not that ugly; he looked like a benign father. He came close and embraced me with emotion. What emotion? The generosity of a victor to his defeated? Not likely. His eyes showed genuine parental love. I did not have to tell him I was leaving. He knew, of course, being so intimate with Dr. Dryle.

My first impression of Dr. Marlowe flashed through my mind.

I had arrived at Urbana on a sunny afternoon. It was nice of Susan to drive me here (she had gotten back from Spain, divorced Jim and married a graduate student; the story of their romance will be carried in *The Atlantic*, this year). I was eager to see the director of graduate studies. But I was one minute late for my appointment because I had been talking with Susan outside. His secretary simply announced: "Dr. Marlowe is ready to go home. You have to wait for an appointment tomorrow." Susan went directly to Marlowe, trying to put in a word for me. Of course, Marlowe was annoyed. Dear me, seeing an authority in America is like seeing an emperor. The anarchist way of catching your boss during a meal won't do in America. It is a free land but extremely well disciplined. If you want to play the game, you must learn the rules.

The following day I met him at his office punctually. When I mentioned that Susan wanted to apply for the job advertised in the department bulletin, he chuckled maliciously.

"Do you think she will have a chance here? I am on the committee."

I did not apply for doctoral study at University of Illinois. Do you think I would have a chance with Dr. Dryle on the committee? I slipped a gift copy of my MA thesis under the door of Dr. Dryle's office and left the English Building.

ON FINISHING . . .

It's finished
I'm Finished
We are not
Shall I fix a Chinese feast?
How about a drink?
Yes, I know you won't come
It's not good enough for a toast of red wine—
Just acceptable, tolerable, okay. . .
Hold the charioteer of your landsliding brain
Use that soft glow of the multi-colored snow
To capture the collapsing beauty of
An Avalanche

free-zing
pure
ruthless
submissively-
wild
A-musing
murky
bitterless
lugubriously-
mild

So little to feel day to day
  So much to ruminate before night
    What accidentally gained cannot be lost
      Adieu!
        No see?
          Not again?
She's soundly lunatic,
    saintly insane,
      deadly mad,
        madly dead

Forget it
> *forget me*
>> *forget you*
>>> *forget her. . . us.*

We Chinese are a loving and tolerant people. We tolerate perhaps because we are weak. Everything can be forgotten; every sin can be forgiven. But my own plagiarism will be the scarlet letter "P" on my breast.

> *It is time to leave*
> *Flowers bloomed and gone*
> *Green of trees comes back*
> *Drizzle again, storm again*
> *Window with a view, yet nothing new*
> *The suitcase, bottom up*
> *Every dress worn, no difference, nothing to show*
> *Urbana-Champaign has lost its glamor*
> *Go, go, go. . . the sparrow chirps*
> *Go, go, go. . .the cold wind whistles*
> *It's time to part! An old ragged car blows its horn.*

I got into a shabby car and left gloomy Urbana. Where am I going? One night Mr. Ma, representing humility and tolerance like my husband, appeared in my dream. He said to me: "Come home! It is a waste of your life to be away from home, your real career." Yes, if I had not left China I would have been a professor by now, and perhaps Chair of the department. The other night I had an entirely different dream. Two tall buildings on fire. Nothing collapses. Fire dragons dancing on the roof touching the sky, tongues of flames licking upwards in the air. I did not know why I was running away. I did not know why I was stopped by a large crowd of strangers, like a scene in a Moses adventure. They shouted to me: "Turn your back and look." Aren't they magnificent? Only a coward runs away.

It was true if I returned to China now I would be thought a coward. Perhaps all of my life I would have to swallow the shame of being a failure. I had never recognized my failure in doing anything before. I was grateful to Professor Millar. He asked me one day what I was planning to do after completing my MA, I said, return to China.

"Why go back to China? I read a couple of your papers. They are good and have a style, too. You should get your PhD. If you are not happy with U. of I., there are many other universities in the States. I will write recommendation letters for you. Please try and never give up."

Stepping out of his office I saw an ad for the Comparative Literature Department at University of Pittsburgh. During a visit to Pitt two years before, Jim had said to me: "A great university. I hope you can do your PhD here." It was my fate. Now the old car was shipping me to Pitt.

=
7
=

Dear Sister, you asked me why I always called myself an ugly duckling in China. I never told you the story of my childhood. Do you still remember how we became sworn sisters on the farm? It was truly laughable. That day I heard a girl wailing in the dorm. I went in and watched you for a long time. Instead of persuading you to stop, I lay down by your side, howling together with you. When we had our fill of crying, we asked each other why we were crying. I said I did not know, perhaps something about the mystery of life; you said, Yes, the pain of living itself. We took a walk and you told me how your parents loved you and had high expectations of you. You cried partly because you felt you had not done anything meaningful in life. Then we took many walks along the mountain path and talked about our dreams, shared our secrets, and pictured our futures. Once or twice we said how wonderful it would be if one of us were a man so that we could marry each other. But I never said a word about my childhood, because it was different.

My life is a dustball rolling, rolling, rolling. When it rolls in the middle of the busy street, all the traffic stops.

I was born at the wrong time in the wrong family. If my birth had occurred twenty years later, my parents would have known the advantage of having an only child. With a brother and a sister ahead of me, I lost all of their love. With three sisters and one brother after me, I was born a free babysitter. I drank no milk nor do I remember the warmth of a maternal arm. Opening my eyes, I saw injustice and hardness of life everywhere.

"Ma . . . My little. . .little sister fell into . . ." When my mother ran home and found a baby howling in the smoldering charcoal fire, she cried helplessly. When my father came, he slapped my face like lightning slashing the clouds.

" Yun" means cloud—that's me, either a dustball along the street or a cloud wandering in the sky. The three-year-old me was certainly too dumb to stop my sister Min from tumbling off the bed or to drag her from the fire.

"Why can't I ride on the back seat of your bike, Pa?" Seeing my brother straddling the front bar, I was deeply hurt by a strong feeling I did not know how to name. No answer, but the sting of an eagle eye, the face of a sullen sky were too much for a little soul. I did not know where my courage came from. I threw my tiny body right in the middle of the boulevard before the Zhengzhou February 7th Memorial Tower, screaming, rolling like a ball of dust. Policemen were stunned, the traffic lights lost their authority, and all trucks, buses, cars screeched to a stop.

The windless summer evening was suffocating. Yet, my heart was light like a breeze. After washing dishes and seeing that the little ones had a clean bath, I finally pulled a fragment of an old mat, like an ant towing a leaf, to my earthly paradise along the sidewalk.

Already many people were there; some sat on small stools or armchairs, while some lay on their mats on sidewalks. What fun people had in a time when nobody knew air conditioning or even electric fans! The old and young were equally relaxed and idle, waving their palmleaf fans.

Grandpa Liu was always the center of attention. Naked to the waist, blowing out from his stubby beard like a young goat, he was telling an old story about Bao Gong, a man of law and justice.

I was fascinated by Bao Gong, though his face was painted rather scarily in black on the stage and he was always flipping his bushy long beard and staring through his round eyes. Grandpa Liu convinced me that only Bao Gong dared to throw off his black official cap and chop the heads off evil governors, even if they were Emperor's relatives. He earned his fame as "Bao the Blue Sky." A child or a woman could stop his sedan chair in the street, crying for justice.

"Do you know anything about Bao Gong's birth?"
I did not know why I was so curious to find out his roots.
"Of course I know." Grandpa Liu's goat beard was erect with pride. "Bao Gong was born a fleshball. When the ball tumbled out of his mother's womb, rolling on the floor, his father cut it open with a long sword and found a dark-skinned ugly baby inside. The father thought it a disgrace for the family and sent

a servant to throw it into the wilderness . . . ."

My mind wandered away. Whether little Bao was fed by wolves in the mountains or farmers in a small cottage, and how he became the Minister of Justice at Kaifeng Court, I did not care any more. I was lost in my own thoughts: If the Emperor himself was an evil tyrant, what could Bao Gong have done? Black—ball, ball—black. A sort of weird ugliness stroked my heart gently. *Ah, people call me an ugly duckling because I was born black with a sense of justice.* For the first time I felt I had a secret link with somebody. And I began to doubt my own parentage.

Another day, something unfair happened. For a toy? No, the children in my family never had toys to play with. For candy? No, I was never spoiled enough to have such an extravagant craving. Anyway, something struck me as unfair, so I refused to eat supper. I wept in big sobs in the dark corner of a room, rather than crying openly like a child. I was thinking about where my blood parents were. Late that night, my father shouted at me: "If you think you are wronged in this family, you can leave." Yes, I must leave. What do I have in this family? I suddenly realized that being a citizen, I should have some identity. I howled: "Give me my Book of Food Rations and my citizenship registration and I will go."

I ran away from home several times and each time I was brought back by the police.

I felt my school was boring too; today a Red Army Man told you how they had chewed grassroots during their Long March and tomorrow an old poor peasant would teach you how to swallow the bitter wild plants as they did in the dark society. So I played truant and fought with boys in the neighborhood. No doubt I became the ugliest among the seven children in the family. Not only my parents often cursed me, but the neighbors joined the chorus. After washing off a day's dust, I watched myself intensely in the mirror and started to compose a tale.

Once upon a time a little rabbit was born. Her parents did not like her because she was ugly. Her brothers got better food and her sisters wore more beautiful clothes. She had nothing but leftovers and hand-me-downs. All day long she was alone, playing with mud. One day

after a big storm the lake looked murky and then crys-
tal clear. The rabbit happened to see her image for the
first time. She marveled: My parents always say I am
ugly. Why do I look so much like my father? Why do I
look so much like my mother? And why do I look so
much like every other rabbit? If they are not ugly in the
first place, how could I ever have been born ugly?

The image of my father was, no doubt, of a tyrant. Many bits
of evidence flash in my memory. The whole family sat around
the dining table waiting for his appearance like waiting for a
dinner bell—but this bell never had a fixed time. If one dish
was burned or salty, my father's finger would fly to peck my
mother's brow. A scene—an indelible imprint—on my mind:

A Cock-pecked Wife

He has a finger
A finger of Baton
>   *directs the traffic of a hen*
>>   *with seven chicks*
>   *crossing the tightrope of life*
A finger of Eye
>   *flares up at first sight of No*
A finger of Cock
>   *pecks the wrinkled brow of the Other*
When His carrot-face grows
>   *black, or purple.*

Of course, a tyrant has the complete freedom to brag about his
merits. Even his shortcomings or defects would become something worth glorifying, if they were recounted by his own mouth.
My father was a peasant. He was used to being thrifty and hard-
working. "Splitting a penny to use it twice" would be an apt de-
scription for him. He was the sole breadwinner for seven children and a wife and he could not afford to have anyone in the
family lose a cent. The children were naturally always penniless. If my mother lost a dollar during her shopping, she would
be scared and such a secret was usually too heavy for her alone
to bear. She would tell her daughters: "Bad luck. I lost a dollar
today. Do not let your father know." No one wanted to be an in-
former anyway. Who liked to see the pots and bowls broken
again?

Once my father came back from a provincial convention and announced: "Bad times indeed! So many thieves are milling around the railway station. One even stole seven dollars from my hip pocket." My father said this with such good humor that we all laughed. My brother was even curious to learn how a thief possibly could steal from a pocket so tight to his hip.

My father joined the Communist army to fight the Japanese when he was fourteen.

"You know, then I was a pigherd for a landlord in the village. One day the son of the landlord bullied me and I gave him a good beating. I dared not return to them any more and ran away to fight the Japanese devils. . . ."

He related many tales about his battles. Once he was carrying a wounded Japanese devil after the battle and the tough devil almost bit his ear off. Though he won the war against Japan, he seemed to admire their unyielding spirit a lot.

Many times he escaped when his comrades-in-arms died in an enemy-surrounded house or village. He was known as the Flying Tiger. He jumped from roof to roof as if stepping on two clouds. He won numerous awards and was promoted time and time again. After recounting his glorious past, he would say wistfully: If I had had a better education, I would be somebody in the Center Party Committee now.

Surely, his glorious past implanted the image of a legendary hero in the children's eyes. But I felt uneasy listening to his never-finished tales. Too many repetitions and too much revision will make any tale lose its color and reliability. The first time, I was as thrilled as the other children. After the third time, I simply slipped away as my father was starting. Later, even before he started, I made faces and snorted a sort of disgust, making myself even more ugly. After seeing Lu Xun's *New Year's Sacrifice* in a movie house, I said to my father before he started the old tale again: "I am so foolish I did not know the wolf would come out in the snow days. I let Ah Mao sit outside. . . ."[4] All my brothers and sisters laughed. My father was puzzled like a twenty-foot-high Buddhist statue, too tall to touch his own head. He clenched his teeth: "Get out, you ugly thing!"

---

[4] In the movie, when Aunt Xianglin first tells how her son was devoured by a wolf, the villagers listen with sympathy and tears; but because she tells the same story too many times, her audience tries to escape before she starts.

=
8
=

Dear Sister, I did have a safe trip. In an old, shabby car, it took two days to jolt from Urbana to Pittsburgh. I could not tell whether it was safe till the minute I got out of the car. I had felt sexually threatened the first day and night. But my driver, Marios, turned out to be a rare noble man. I must tell you our story and his own stories.

"Hi, Liu. I am leaving Urbana soon."

"When?"

"I am going to buy a Greyhound ticket. Hopefully the day after tomorrow."

"Where?"

"Pittsburgh. A city near Philadelphia, I guess."

" Well, good luck to you. My friend Marios happens to be leaving for Philadelphia tomorrow afternoon. I believe he can give you a ride."

"Is Marios a man?" I hesitated.

"Yes, a Greek man. If there's one man you can trust in the world, it is him." Liu laughed with confidence.

"Sounds great."

"Here's his phone number."

I phoned immediately. No answer. A few measures of Beethoven were followed by a cheerful announcement.

"This is Marios. I am not home at the moment. Please leave your phone number and I shall call you back as soon as possible." The voice was open and resolute, reminding me of the image of a young Greek warrior.

When he finally came to get me and my belongings the following morning, I was shocked to see a huge man, with a scar crossing his face. I was instantly frightened. Edward had told me, "If you pay the gas and half of the motel, if you stay, I don't think he will take advantage of you."

It was too late to retreat. I got into the car and he drove me first to his dwelling in the basement of an old building. He asked me to help prepare some food for the journey. He looked clumsy like a bear but did not cook slowly. We fried a big bag of chicken drumsticks and prepared some sandwiches. He had already bought a lot of candies and soft drinks.

"I have diabetes. I need a lot of liquid and food when I am driving."

I was not really clear about diabetes then. But it added to my fear: now I was traveling with a savage man with a disease.

We set out by four o'clock in the afternoon. As our car was backing out of the yard, a lot of young men waved goodbye to him. No doubt, he was a popular hero among them.

Marios was in an exceptionally good mood. He turned on his car music. Again, classical.

"You don't like pop music, I bet."

"No, that's low stuff. I have inherited a sensitive ear from my father, who was a great singer and my grandfather who was a famous composer. Unfortunately, my own voice is not suitable for professional singing. But thanks to my good ear, I can still enjoy music and repair fine musical instruments."

After a while Marios started whistling. It was the most beautiful whistling I had ever heard in my life. It was not thin, but a double, triple echoing.

"How can you do that?"

"Eh, a family trait. I come from an aristocratic family in Greece. All the males in my family can do double-whistling."

"You mean your family in Greece is extremely rich. Then why did you come to America?" At the point of asking him why he looked so shabby and his car was so old, I held my tongue.

"Well, we used to be. Nevertheless, it is the belief that a man must go out to see the world and get experience: this belief took me to America. I am a man of strong will. When I was small, I was the weakest in the family, always sick and bullied by my brothers. Then I was determined to make myself strong. I did hard training. Look at all these muscles. Look into my eyes. Do you find some strange light? I can see into the distance far-ther than most other human eyes.

"Although I dress in rags, I am not terribly poor, compared with poor Americans. I am a mechanic, earning 17 dollars an hour. I give 20 bucks to a single mother with a baby near the campus every week. It makes me feel good to help the helpless a little."

Is he telling me stories? Can he be that good to an unrelated woman? Perhaps that woman's baby is his illegitimate son.

"Who is that man in the house?"

"His name is Edward, the host of the family I have lived

with for about a year."

"No problem. You are a desirable woman."

What does he mean? Is he suspecting an intimate relationship between me and Edward? He is dangerously penetrating.

"That lady in the house has an STD."

"Oh, she's a visitor, one of Edward's women friends. What is an STD?"

"A sexually transmitted disease."

"How could you tell?"

"Well, I just know."

"She is an abandoned woman with three little kids. Edward pities her. Edward has pity for many women."

"No problem. Edward is a ladies' man."

Now I knew "No problem" was his pet phrase.

"Do you know Minghua, a beautiful Chinese graduate student?"

"Sorry, I don't."

"Ha, ha, ha—She calls me 'Mental Disorder.'"

He must be in love with her. A beautiful woman could play around with an ugly man or a dwarf for fun and bless him with all sorts of cruel names, but she would not give him her love.

"'Mental Disorder.' How do you say it in Chinese?"

"Shenjing Bing." A lot of Chinese women call their stupid admirers by that name.

"I guess I am a Shenjing Bing. Now I am sending this car to her in Philadelphia at her command. She bought this old car at my advice for only three hundred dollars. Good engine, though its body looks shabby."

Marios drank some soda and ate a chocolate bar.

He sang a tune I did not understand. It must be in his mother tongue.

"My father died ten years ago. My mother used to have hysteric fits. When I became a man, I came to understand women better. Two years ago I went to London and bought some sexual aids from a sex store for her. Since then, she has changed to a much milder person in the house."

"When I saw signs of sex shops in London, I assumed that they had something to do with underground prostitution."

"No. It is a kind of health shop. There are instruments for men, too. I did not buy one for myself as I am still young and there are women who like to use me."

"Use you?"

"Yes. Sex, love, and marriage are separate and different

things. I have regular sex with a U. of I. faculty member. We
see each other twice a month, nothing except for a physical need.
We did not even ask each other's names. She needs what I need.
We are glad to use each other for a healthy existence.
Repression of sex is no good, against our biological nature. . . . I
am not ready for marriage yet. Marriage is sacred. It is for the
sake of our future generations. The mother of my kids has to be
refined, virtuous, well-educated. . . ."

He was dreaming of a goddess, perhaps modeled on his view
of his own mother.

He did not talk about his philosophy of love. But "Mental
Disorder" had laid him bare.

It was well past midnight. He started yearning. I knew we
had to spend a night in a hotel. Thinking of the hotel, I became
pretty tense.

"You are a desirable woman." He gave me a critical
glance.

"But do not get nervous. If you do not want to make love with
me, I won't touch you. But I confess I desired your body the moment I saw you."

"Can we sleep in separate hotel rooms?"

"I think it's too expensive to pay for two rooms. If you are
worried, I can sleep in the car. I am a tough man and have slept
in the car several times."

I thought of Liu's trust for him.

"All right. We can share the room. But you must keep your
promise."

That night we slept on the same bed. I did not undress myself. But it was summer and my silk dress was vulnerably
thin. At first I struggled to keep awake to protect myself from
him. I could hear him turning his body like an ant on a hot pan.
I was hopelessly carsick. Gradually I lost consciousness.
When I woke up, I heard him in the shower.

"It was so hot last night I simply could not fall asleep."

With the air conditioning on, the room was not hot. I knew
he had fought with his carnal desire the whole night. He had
won the victory, but was terribly exhausted.

The following day, he drove silently. Sometimes he whis-
tled, but the tune was unspeakably depressing. I tried once or
twice to cheer him up. It was of no use. He simply said, "I did
not sleep well and I am tired."

Do you still remember I sent you a poem on sex and love
about eight months ago? Let me repeat it here:

Sex Is Love

Who says sex is not love?
To me
    Sex is love as beauty is truth
When sex and love are separated
    sex stinks
        love deceives
            soul tortures

A momentary release
    An eternal trauma

Sex should be the highest form of love—
Love ennobles and purifies sex
Sex electrifies ecstatic love

Sex without love
    signifies weakness of human will—
A yield to vulva itching
or a capitulation to phallic power
A mere tool for breeding offspring
or a victim of the material world.

Marios was a post-modern specter sent to instruct me to separate sex from love, but I failed to take his instruction. Even though my body was profaned, my spirit demoralized, and I was driven out of the Garden of Eden as a plagiarist, I still stubbornly held to the last straw: sex, given of one's free will, is love.

Sex =/= Love ?

Yun arrived at Pittsburgh like a patient discharged from the mental hospital. She shunned social life and concentrated on getting straight A's. If she was dragged by her friend Amy to a dance, she would sit in a corner, staring. Once or twice she was pushed by the feminist tide in her department and went along with a couple of strong women to a hen party. While they were talking about divorce, love, sex, and fantasies, Yun remained a mute onlooker. Between busy hours of course work and teaching, she felt depressed and lonely in an alien world. The Chair had a talk with her and advised her to wear a bra because a graduate student had reported she dressed too sexily. Yun seldom wore a bra in the winter because her clothes were thick enough to hide her pointed nipples. But one must be careful in a sex-alert world like America. In China, some women wear translucent dresses in summer without slips. The dumb Chinese men are blind to the women's bodies. Perhaps both sexes enjoy seeing and being seen secretly. But no talking—the words are the real criminals.

One day a voice behind Yun commented, "Great legs." She turned and saw a well-dressed gentleman. She laughed rather coarsely and he hurried away in embarrassment. Perhaps he was not embarrassed but took her as a crazy woman. She was told that in that situation a woman should smile and say, "Thank you." It was not that easy to fit into a different culture.

One evening after she crossed the street facing the campus entrance, she was accosted by a dark shadow.

"Ha, it's you. Do you still remember me?" Yun looked but could not remember him.

"Sorry, you must have made a mistake."

"Never mind. I used to have an Asian girlfriend. She is a

wonderful Korean girl. Are you Korean?"

"No. I'm Chinese."

"I love Chinese food. Are you married?"

"Yes, I have a child, too."

"Is your family with you?"

"Excuse me, I must leave. My husband and daughter are waiting for me at home." Having a family seems to protect a woman.

One night when a friend dropped her off at the intersection near her apartment, she heard a man calling from his lowered car window.

"Please tell me how to get to Hugh Street."

Yun told him patiently.

"I am a stranger in this town. I've been driving around and can't get to the right place. Would you please get in and show me the way?"

Yun knew the the misery of getting lost in a strange place. So she got in. What a fool she was. No sooner was the car moving than the man asked, "Do you swallow?"

"What?"

"Swallow."

Yun knew the word in English but could not figure out what he meant. Nevertheless, she knew instinctively he was a bad man. When he tried to touch her hand, she said sharply, "Let me out." Her voice must have sounded foreign and authoritative. The man was scared and let her out immediately. Yun ran home, feeling threatened, as if she could see a woman being assaulted every minute, every second, in the world. Perhaps not. An older lady in China had told her that it was impossible for a man to rape a woman without her complicity. Perhaps it is true; but a woman must be physically as strong as a man. She recalled once a man had attempted to assault her; she pushed him down to the ground and ran away. Having labored in the countryside for three years, she was strong, although her voice and figure still looked pretty feminine. Well, if you asked Yun what she feared most about walking alone in the dark, she would reply: a man, not a ghost.

Yun could recall many temptations. When the most handsome man in her department—most women thought so— squeezed her palm in a handshake, she pretended not to take the hint. They lived on the same floor in the same building for a year. She could easily see that he changed girlfriends like an American's good habit of changing clothes. If Yun was a hidden female Don Juan, she disliked male dandies. After she had just moved to Pitt, a graduate student known as a ladies' man often dropped by her cubicle for a chat. Once he made a comment about her gray hair and even volunteered to pluck some off. Yun was too polite to lose her temper. In no more than two weeks, the department was gossiping about her and him.

—I heard that he invited you to a bar last night.

—No, he didn't.

—Didn't? He does that to every female newcomer in our department.

Strange, he had never invited Yun. He offered her a ride home once but in a most decent manner. Even so, Yun felt irritated and could hardly bear the sight of him. She had been wronged by his reputation. A woman's reputation is more important than her career—when Yun was rational, she believed this. Pretty soon she was known in the department as an "aloofer" who could not get on with life.

Watching Mary and Diana riding on the shoulders of Doug and Bill during a playful game at a party, she wished she could join in. Seeing Tom jump around with two grapefruits as his breasts, she wish she could invent some fun.

How can one get on with life? Is there another way of getting on with life without sexual tantalization? She found some pleasure talking with elderly ladies and men in church. She started enjoying food and fashionable clothes. She even wrote a passage to express her momentary self:

> *I am a woman. My mind is so minute if I think of philosophy or math one minute, my brain rewards myself nine times more in the cosmos of love. I enjoy food, I enjoy clothes, I enjoy window shopping. Why, aren't they the elementals of life? Why should I snail down my squirrel movements like a modern kangaroo—her pocket loaded with not her own baby but others' brainchildren?*
>
> *Did I tell you I am a camel? I eat tons of good food when I get a chance to. "Hello, Yun, do you want to fill up your camel again?" Oh, I am so pleased. I'll go even if tomorrow I lose my chance of being the President. Did I even eat like a parasite? No. I pay with my witty Huism when I am ruminating the fibers. The significance does not lie in the eating.*

Small verbal pleasures never exercised her intellect much. When Yun was annoyed or threatened, she felt the circulation of her blood. When nothing could spur her imaginative power, she started to hunger for pain.

Pain

Coma of Love
Let the locomotive of time shoot
            bursting through a tunnel
But me snug in the eider-down
            sucking Dream's mellow

Let the dead die
Let the dreamer lie

Coming to is being dragged through a boundless swamp
Waking up produces pain by the rusty sawtooth

Life devoid of pain bulges into an anchorless balloon . . .

Pain, a lump of quivering flesh dripping red

Pain!
    Pain!
        My bleached lips gasp

Do the fingernails of pain
        twirl the most beautiful music
            on the zither of nerves?

If God grant me only one wish
I will thrust my arms and cry:
Pain, please condemn me to the infinite pain
            in the eternal grave of love.

=
2
=

How can one inflict personal pain upon herself by not resorting to love? Yun decided to take on the role of a huntress. It so happened that she caught Bob, or Bob caught her, almost without an effort.

"Oh, you got your MA from University of Illinois at Urbana-Champaign. I used to teach at University of Chicago and am quite familiar with U. of I. One year I was invited by their English Department to give a talk. How was your life there?"

"Quite good, except that a professor was annoyed by one of my papers."

"What did you write about?"

"I interpreted Keats' 'To Autumn' as a poetic celebration of female beauty, because of his images of curves, roundness, mellowness, etc. But that professor challenged my lack of discussion of male beauty."

"Ha-ha-ha, male beauty. There's a lot to see on a female body. What can a male body display? Even women like to watch a beautiful female, don't you think so?" A fresh question. Reflecting for a moment, Yun admitted to herself that she was attracted to any true beauty—either female or male. Chinese classical beauty favors feminine smoothness and delicacy; but in recent years the Chinese female aesthetic judgment has been affected by Western taste for hairy and angular features.

"Shall we continue our talk in my apartment tonight?"

Yun liked to talk with him and was instantly enchanted by his eyes. She went to her office and wrote a short poem.

> *A universal being—*
> *No nationality*
> *No sex*
> *No age*
> *All is love flowing up*
> *to a pair of eyes*

That pair
    resolute,   tender
       elite,   down to earth
Inquisitive wonder twinkles
          in an omniscient iris
Two chameleon stars radiate music
          from a cosmic arch.

Reading the little poem a couple of times, Yun felt a yearning for him.

THE SKY
    in utter depression
A sudden swelling of loneliness
       Oh, BOB—SOS!
Who is howling so
          in the walled little cubicle?

The wind is playing the accordion
Dancing cranes sprinkle feminine pearls
A macho tree giraffes its neck
       Higher than Cathedral of Learning's peacock tail
How she wishes she were a tiny bee
          nestling on the heart-platform of
          your lotus boat.

When Yun went to his apartment he showed her the nineteen
books he had published and won great admiration from her.
(Yun recalled a scene that had occurred during a visit to a professor in his office. After showing her all his published books
and poems, that professor had unzipped his pants to display his
huge penis. Yun was bold enough to hold it by hand and deflate
it.) Yun and Bob darted over different subjects. Almost for the
first time Yun felt she was talking to someone who was her
equal. She felt the need to pursue him like Humbert seeking
Lolita. Bob suggested they have dinner in State College the following night.
    It was a drizzling romantic night, but it was difficult to find
a restaurant on the opening day of the football season at Penn
State. Being a man of elegance, Bob was unable to dine at a sec-
ond-rate restaurant. Driving-driving-driving—finally they

stopped at a country tavern and had wonderful salmon there. Back at her apartment, Yun portrayed their experience in a long poem.

Hunting for a Tavern

In the forests of tall stalagmites,
Beasts of cars racing along the glazed trail,
Each hunts with two glaring eyes.

Dear Artemis,
Who are you hunting
A deer, a doe—transfigurations of muse?
Oui, la curiosité tue la femme.

See, that green masterhand
  is hunting for a tavern,
    with pockets of paper gold.

Found. But ooh, la la,
A deflated balloon.
Who knows today is the *carpe diem* of football knights?
No reservation? Wait till after nine.
Non, l'impatience tue l'homme.

Driving, driving
Hush— this one won't do.
See, nobody's inside;
Food must be bad.

Who bothers to discover the epiphyllum
Blushing among broad leaves at a chilly midnight?

Driving, driving
Hush— that one will never do —
 the elegant atmosphere is too alluring.
Hush— not this one —
 the dainty fragrance is still lingering.

Driving, driving— dreary diving —
 the appetizer for one's stomach or
  hot pepper for one's temper?

Pas exactement!
The landslide of an ideal standard.

Ah, this one—Fast & Cheap.
Why not stop here?
No, a long queue.
L'impatience tue l'homme.
You go in and have a look.
Non, la curiosité tue la femme.

Let's get in this one,
        a few shadows blurring in the beaded screens.
The air here distills no celestial tea,
But a nice Jolly Corner, you know,
Which keeps brushing old James' attic membrane.

Ooh, la la,
Hunting in a cemented woods in a rain.
Palate is captured by eager stomach,
Taste tapering into the mushrooms of mist.
Vermilion lips hug an agamogenetic bowl,
Heartily smacking — A-muse.

    One night they talked about eroticism.   Bob asked her
whether she had ever seen a porno movie.
    "No, I haven't."
    "You must see one; otherwise, how can you talk about mod-
ern pornography?"
    They went to see one on campus. Yun was surprised to meet
a couple of graduate students from her department, all unmarried. The movie was full of repetitions. Yun was soon bored.
Bob and she walked back to his apartment. Bob suggested they
do something real. Yun said, perhaps tomorrow. Yun knew that
Bob was largely interested in her body. A long fishing rod was
waiting for that one thing.

Ah, Bald Eagle of America!
Are you going to pick her
        like one of the eye-catching pebbles
            along the beach?

Are you going to touch her
*   as a pink petal in a blossom grove*
*   of peach?*
She wishes to evaporate her youth into your blunt beak
She dreams to iron your wrinkled brow with her warm bosom
In love, she bows her willowy crest below billows

Mind you, dear Bald Eagle
She is no angel but a perch-fairy from the Western Lake
*   Prepared to be left unforgotten —*
*   a Cold Mirage on China sea.*

It was Sunday. Yun jogged with Bob in the woods and then made love to him in his apartment. Although Bob was much older than her father, she felt quite pleasant. She was aware that her love for the old man was more intellectual than sensual. She employed him as her spiritual emancipator.

"Are you coming next week?"

"Yes, I'm coming."

One may possess her body
One may engage her mind
Who can win her love—an elevator to poetic ecstasy?
She is cool to the degree of cruelty
She woos no lover but a catamite muse

Bone without marrow
A stratified stone
Love—the marrow in the stone of life

Hail!
Love, are you coming to rescue the SOS
in the wailing cemetery of a frozen muse?

Yes, I am coming
I am voluntarily coming
I am walking shoulder to shoulder with you
You are not demanding my following

Yes, I feel happy
I am very happy
You are my ideal image
I am to join you
to meet my own communion

Yes, I am thrilled
I am thrilled to greet
my metamorphosed birth—
A stormy petrel soaring out of a caterpillar

Yes, I am free
I am no longer curdled in a cellar
I am off the palm of Rulaifo[1] —
the thousand-hand-and-thousand-eyed Buddha.[2]

Yun was recalling their conversation.   When she mentioned feeling like an equal to Bob, Bob laughed, "How could you be my equal? Perhaps Emma can; she has published 17 books. But her body is ugly." Yun realized that male scholars seldom mixed academics with the body. A famous male scholar generally marries a beauty nameless in, or out of, his field. Lying in bed, Yun felt a tinge of pain. She made up a bedtime story.

BOB

BOB
A cosmic sunbird
Day in and night out
Majestic he looks
Standing on the peak of the Himalayas
Thrusting his saintly chest
Pointing to his sagely head
Proudly he said:

---

[1] Rulaifo is more powerful than all of the gods in Chinese mythology. One somersault of Golden Monkey in *The Journey to the West* covers 108,000 *li* (Chinese mileage, 2 *li* =1 kilometer); yet he is still in the palm of Rulaifo.

[2] When one visits China, one must not miss the Buddha with a Thousand Hands and a Thousand Eyes. It is the symbolic equivalent of the Temple of the Golden Pavilion in Japan.

Wo— Wo— Wo—
My crest is still in good shape!

A lonely tiny lark
Half drowned in her dreams of icicles
Shivering
> *Soaring to the sky:*
Wind, my Great Grand Father
Tell me
Where can I find a bosom friend?

Wo— Wo— Wo—
My crest is still in good shape!

The tiny lark panted on a cliff:
Earth, my Great Grand Mother
Tell me
Where can I find a bosom friend?

Wo— Wo— Wo—
My crest is still in good shape!

The tiny lark
Clung to a shuddering twig
The sun failed to rise
Night succeeded by dark dawn
Suddenly
The Sky cracked its gold whip
Chained fire-dragons shook their flaming scales
> *in wild disco*
The drunken trees madly bumped each other's
> *nipples and hips*

"Little lark, little lark
Come, and dance with me!"
The sunbird invited her, bickering with his crest

"I can't dance—"
Lark's voice was vanishingly thin
A careless nod
She fell to the music-box of the woods.

All animals were having a primal singing contest
Howling and shrieking
Meowing and neighing
Snorting and sneezing
The tiny lark picked herself up from dead leaves
Putting on Heron's crown as her red shoe
There she goes!

The whole sky teemed with ominous chuckles of owls:
Haa— haa— ha—
See, she forgets herself
She can dance on one toe!

The whole world became blurred and blurring
Dragons in the heaven flashing and flashing
Crocodiles in the waters splashing and splashing
She ever cared and she cares no more
She waltzed in the daffodils by the lake
She hopped upon the ruddy billows of sea
She tumbled over blazing fire
She glided through deep freezer
Dionysus ran wild
But failed to find her bosom friend

Wo— Wo— Wo—
My crest is still in good shape!

"How can I ever cross to you—
such an infinite distance
with so little between?"

The tiny lark plunged headlong to the despair
of the humming ocean

In the slumber of death
Her sensitive ear
wistfully heard
the fading of her raven hair
The feet of solitude tapped a funeral lullaby:

Nothing could be held
Even color of black
Scratched a few numb marks

Then stealthily left . . . .

The following weekend when Yun went to his apartment a young woman barred his bedroom door because Bob was making a telephone call. Bob told her that the woman had been his girlfriend for the past two years. He wanted to have romance tonight with both of them. Yun was shocked and refused to engage in a *ménage à trois*. But she agreed to take photos for them. She did select some good shots with an artist's eye. When she was leaving, Bob said to her, "We are decent people, aren't we?" Yes. They were quite a decent, graceful couple. Yun could tell how the woman loved him in a cute, kittenish way. One should not demand that every woman be a feminist. The feminine has her own beauty. It should be a personal choice, perhaps.

Now Yun was clear about her own relationship with Bob: two players.

> *When I loved you*
> > *your love carried away my lost body*
> *When I hate you*
> > *an intensive care is scorching my own heart*
> *The time, perhaps, will soon arrive*
> > *at a numbed indifference —*
> *Blind as Night to galloping clouds*
> *Deaf as Mountains to the bellowing sea*
> *Two mute players part, without pain,*
> > *after a sandcastle game.*

Bob left Pittsburgh to teach in Brazil. At Christmastime, he sent a greeting card to Yun and she sent him "Athena's Report to Apollo":

> *Rain shed its fisheggs*
> *Wind has lost its drive*
> *All gone*
> > *When snow melts*
> *Two hoops roll apart*
> *On a chilly ground.*

To explain the poem, she also made up a Christmas Story.

Artemis and Apollo join their lights once in a million days. The moment they catch each other's loving eyes they are parting. Artemis says to Apollo:

> *"You are passing me because*
> *you love to shed light on too many.*
> *When you are gone, my heart aches,*
> *my feelings jumble, and my fingers juggle.*
> *Please take my heart with you*
> *   to recreate the yolk of your round body.*
> *I'll be heartless and be forever happy.*
> *Please take my feelings with you*
> *   to renew your morning rays.*
> *I'll be feelingless and no filaments*
> *   tangle my feet.*
> *Please take my rosy fingers with you*
> *I'll be fingerless and never touch*
> *   Dawn's gray belly. "*
> *As she is speaking, her body vanishes*
> *Her face turns into one eye—*
> *   the bright eye of Athena.*
> *As Apollo is listening,*
> *He chuckles himself into Santa Claus*
> *   in red and white.*
> *He makes toys out of human hearts and feelings*
> *To trigger off merry laughter*
> *   beyond the power of solar light.*

> *Green are the wood parasols*
> *Red paints daisy bells*
> *Yellow-dyed daffodils twist their thighs*
> *   flirting with the blue sky*

> *A hundred chuckles gurgle in an owl's throat—*
> *   seeing Artemis' amorous eye caught by*
> *   a hobbling stag.*

However, Yun loved Bob as her most respected teacher, not
only in academics but in the art of love. Bob was a most innocent man, almost like a baby. A couple of months later, she even
wrote him a playful verse:

The smooth vase of a nineteen
The urchin twinkle of a twenty
Ah, a pair of dreamers!
Holding to a timeless rose
Swing in the waltz of innocence
Can we ever grow old
When age fled from our Milky Way?

=
3
=

When Yun finally cut off the link between sex and love, she felt a never-tasted relaxation.

Friday afternoon when she was looking for an apartment, she met a young man named Sun in front of an ancient-looking building covered with ivy that resembled Medusa's hair. He told her that there was a vacancy on the first floor and offered to move her stuff in his car. As Yun did not have a car, she took the offer without hesitation.

After she moved into the old building on Saturday, she felt quite excited. Her apartment was extremely spacious, a lot of holes—sun room, study den, closets with doors here and there—and a surprisingly large sitting room. It was Yun's habit to reward those who helped her with a homemade dinner. She was not so generous that she would give her helper an expensive treat in a restaurant. Nor was she a terrible miser. Being a tolerable cook, she enjoyed cooking to her imaginative diversity.

Sunday evening Sun came to her apartment and they dined together most properly and had delightful little talks between chewing and swallowing. When they were full of the feast, the dishes on table seemed to have been hardly touched. The refrigerator was going to be stuffed like a turkey and she could live on leftovers for at least a week.

Sun was lingering. When he finally lifted a foot to go he suddenly said, "We haven't had our last course, have we?"

"What course? Dessert? Ice cream? Sorry, I forgot to buy it as it does not generally go with a Chinese menu."

"No. I mean sex."

"Oh? That!" Yun was astonished, but she recovered in a minute. It felt funny to hear a young man, a Chinese, being so frank. So she was not annoyed.

" Well, I will think it over and let you know tomorrow. "

Sun left like a guilty little boy. Yun tried hard to think about him. Nothing came to her mind—no image, no image at all. He was a plain man, indeed, if not ugly. But he was young. What was his last mumbling? A virgin? A man of 28 still a virgin? How does a male virgin affect the psychology of a woman? She thought of her stupid husband remaining a virgin after sleeping with her for a dozen days. She thought of Meng's wistful words: "I should have made love with you before your marriage. I have never tasted a virgin." Meng's agonized look convinced Yun that if he did not deflower a woman in his life, he could not shut his eyes on his deathbed.

The following day Sun came to her apartment with a schoolbag on his shoulder. His humble and eager look made Yun feel cruel to say no. Does LeGuin say sex can be a gesture of pity or compassion, a gift for a friend, a release of tension?

He was a virgin. The budding relationship with a woman should be pure, not profaned. Yun said, "Tomorrow is my birthday." It was perhaps a lie. How could she have a birthday any time she wanted?

Sun invited her eagerly, "Let's celebrate your birthday at Peking Garden in Harrisburg."

"How far away is Harrisburg? Two hours' drive? Okay."

At about eleven that night Yun heard someone knocking at the door. It was freezing outside. Who's coming for a visit at this hour of the night? It was Sun, with a bouquet of darkred roses in his stiff hand. She let him in to warm himself for a second before chasing him back out into the cold. Yun saw that there wasn't a card in the bouquet. No need, anyway. If he wrote anything about love, he would become a contemptible object of hypocrisy. He was starved. He was begging for sex. His hands touched his tightened pants nervously, but he would have to suffer and wait.

Yun and Sun dressed up for the special occasion. On the way to Harrisburg Yun teased him and encouraged him to talk about anything he wanted. Dirty jokes, scandals. . . Okay. One minute Yun giggled like a little girl; another minute she guffawed like a vulgar man. Sun felt perfectly relaxed and he even showed her the perfumed picture of a nude blond he kept for his secret pleasure.

"Peking Duck, Sweet and Sour Pork, Mongolian Beef. . . ."

"That's enough," Yun cut off Sun's order crisply.

They ate, drank, and talked. Almost for the first time Yun acted as a listener. She learned that in his spare time Sun played cards, read and watched pornography, masturbating. With a group of Chinese men, he even went to New York and paid to touch a part of a female body.

"You can't see the face. She is blocked by sliding opaque

glass. If you pay $2 you may look at her nipple; if you pay $5 you may look at her beneath; if you pay $10, you may touch. . . finger. . . ."

Yun was absolutely shocked, then unshocked. This is America, a free world.

Yun finished her dinner and suddenly had a yearning for something.

"May I have an ice cream cone?" She had forgotten her own wallet in the car.

"Yes, sure!" Sun was happy, like a mixture of a father and a little child.

The spiral chocolate cone came. Yun took it over feeling like the Statue of Liberty holding a torch. Then the torch started to drip. Its image changed into something Yun was afraid of seeing—the spraying male organ while a female licked, an image from the only porno movie she had watched with Bob. Then the image changed again—a male was sucking the nipple covered with heavy cream in a Japanese movie called *Tampopo*. Sex=food. She felt unable to eat the ice cream any more.

"Quick, it's dripping. Let me have a bite." Sun's mouth poked over and bit off almost half of the cone. Then Yun and Sun had mouthfuls in turn. Yun recalled that two of her best students in Wuda had been rejected by the university as teachers simply because they were seen eating from one bowl on campus. But this was America. There was nothing to fear. And the people around them did not even give them a glance.

"Shall we stay in a hotel tonight?" Sun suggested with some confidence.

"I am busy writing a paper tonight. Wait until another time. Moreover, we are so near campus that I cannot tolerate a hotel room; nor can I tolerate our own apartments with detective Chinese eyes around."

Sun was a smart boy. He planned everything for a weekend trip to Seaworld in Ohio.

"I have seen Seaworld three times before with the guys. But this time, with you, everything here looks fresh and interesting."

"Really? I hooked a trout," Yun said rather unhappily, because the angling contest had absolutely no meaning. It took skill not to hook one in a small pool overcrowded with fish.

"The dolphin's performance is superb." Yun took a picture of the jumping angel. *A dolphin is said to be a most intelligent mammal. What's the use of her intelligence except in offering onlookers a little more pleasure?*

Finally they got into a hotel room. Sun became too excited and his nervousness turned Yun into a shy virgin. After all, Sun was a man. When he finally gathered his courage to press Yun onto the bed to kiss her, she pushed him away. After taking a shower she lay beneath the white sheet, waiting. He was taking a shower. In a minute he would be invading her realm nude. She was not afraid but felt the mysterious air surrounding the room. He turned off the light before he came to her. *An old hand. He does not need any teaching.* They made love gently. Yun turned on the light and discovered how ugly his body was: something like a tree scar snarling in his belly.

"Oh, that? When I was a child I had many worms and had an operation."

"Dear me!" She could see knots of worms wriggling from that hole even now.

"Do you notice my upper body is long and broad? My mother, sisters, and the rest of the family respect me enormously because my heart is larger and I am exceptionally intelligent."

"Your family respect you because you have a larger heart? How could they see your heart?" Yun laughed in good humor. She forgot his ugliness. They made love again, more vigorously. Nowadays it is so easy for contemporary Chinese to sing that sex is beauty. Nobody feels that the body is ugly anymore. Even if a body is ugly, that ugliness merely belongs to that individual. It will not infect the other.

During springtime, dawn visits the window early but the lovers always wake up late. Yun was finally stirred by a lusty stroking. They released their last gust of wind and rain. When the roused waves relaxed into gentle ripples, Sun smacked his lips and chewed a Tang poem deliciously:

> *A spring dreamer never knows the coming dawn,*
> *only to be wakened by the warbling birds.*
> *After a nightful din of the wind and rain,*
> *Who can tell how many flowers have fallen ?*

"You see, this poem is extremely sexy. Meng Haoran was not merely depicting nature, he alluded to the fall of numerous deflowered maidens after a spring orgy of the wind and rain. . . ."

Yun was known for her poetic sensitivity but had never gotten such an insight from that poem. She was enlightened by his
reading. Right, he is right. Lin Daiyun laments the fate of
falling flowers and buries them beneath pure earth, to avoid
their dismembered petals being tramped into the mud. But Yun
could not help laughing at the situational irony—he, not she, had
been deflowered by the night.

"Why are you laughing?"

"Nothing."

They had patches of pleasure week after week. They experi-
mented with all sorts of ways of making love: oral and anal,
you on top of me and I on top of you. . . . Apart from these bodily
experiments, they created a whole discourse of sex and love of
their own. When they felt the roof was too confining, they made
love in the forest and by the lake.

"If caught by the police, we have to pay a $300 fine."

"Really?" This country was not really as free as China.
Yun was thinking about the crops pressed down here and there in
the fields and intertwined bodies in the bushes of Zhongshan
Park. But true love always involves an act that is illegal. The
restriction at least gave them illicit pleasure.

Physical love is never enough for a relationship. They enjoyed talking about every subject they knew: poetry, art, pornography, mathematics, scientific inventions, astrology, the fate of
China. . . . Some mornings Sun snuck into her apartment with
hot dumplings that he had steamed himself. Some nights Yun
cooked Chinese delicacies to see him off on an errand. They felt
that nothing was trivial or vulgar. Love and family life were
never left out of their topics.

"If I get this job in Florida, would you come and see me every
month?"

"If my airplane crashed, could you put a bunch of fresh flowers on my tomb every year on the Chinese memorial day?"

"I know some day I would become a character in your novel.
Please be kind with your pen."

Writing a novel? Something like *Lady Hu and Her Lovers*?
She knew his desire to have their romance perpetuated in words.

"I wish I could marry your younger sister, if you had one."

"I have three sisters, all married and each with a child."

"If you are pregnant, please do not have an abortion. I would
support the child. I want to have a child with you."

"Sorry. I have a child and I am too busy to have another

one."

"I'll take care of it, or perhaps we can put it with a foster family. . . ."

"Nonsense. You are young and you should get married and have your own child."

"Have you heard the campus gossip about my fiancée?"

"Yes."

"Why haven't you asked me about it?"

"Why should I, since it's your own business? However, I am curious to know why you sent her away."

"Well, she is quite pretty, a smart girl. She came to Pittsburgh to marry me. God knows why she behaved so strangely when she arrived. She kept phoning a 'foreigner' who had taught in her college in China. The neighbors and my pals all egged me on to send her back to China. Finally, I did. She was disgusting, wasn't she? She merely wanted to use me to come to the U.S. Once she was here, she tried to get in touch with her previous lover, I guess. But, you know, Americans are law-abiding people and they dare not steal a woman who has already signed marriage papers with another man. So her lover refused her."

"What happened to her when she was sent back to China?"

"She was abandoned by her family. She lost her job. . . ."

Yun was no longer listening. She knew that the girl had been ostracized by society. No men wanted her and no women had sympathy for her. She wept day and night. Finally, she drank DDV poison and died.

"No. I've never heard that she is dead."

"Yes, I know she is dead. You killed her." Yun felt extremely sad. Why can't a girl have a moment of fantasy before she yields to the ugly reality? You think you men are righteousness personified. You sent her to her death. But look at yourself. You are debasing yourself with a married woman without a shred of shame. Yun knew when she left him that he would marry a young girl—a virgin.

Yun was struck by their last conversation and could no longer be with him.

Before long Sun had a young girlfriend.

Perhaps that girl constantly tormented herself over her prospective fall to ugly reality and often released her tension in fits of temper. Sun wanted to return to Yun, but she cleverly shunned him. At a party, Yun told his girlfriend that a human being should be judged by his qualities, not by mere looks. Although Sun had not found a job yet, he had intelligence and

capability. Sun told Yun one day that his girlfriend left him because she had heard that Yun and he had spent a night together
in Ohio.

Yun looked into his eyes sternly.

"I never went with you anywhere. I've never been to Ohio."

"You. . ." Sun was stunned.

The following day Sun and his girlfriend were formally en-
gaged. Yun was neither happy nor unhappy—she repaid him as
her former lover but failed to avenge that innocent girl he had
abandoned to death. Revenge is simply not in the nature of a
woman who has been a mother.

Reflecting upon her relationship with Sun, Yun felt a pleas-
antness that accelerated the fluid of her body but produced no intensity for poetry. She recognized the beauty in bodily contact itself; every contact with a new body was not a simple repetition
but a book review. No matter how dull a book it was, if you read
into it you would learn something.

=
4
=

After she had separated herself from Sun, Yun made "acciden-
tal" love to a couple of men on campus. While she was teaching
an intensive Chinese course during the summer, she mentioned
in one class that she had not seen the Statue of Liberty. When the
summer session ended, a student in his late 20s named Tony offered to drive her to New York for sightseeing. Tony was not the
most brilliant student, but was certainly the most decent-look-
ing and considerate person in the whole class. Yun happily accepted. Since Tony worked at Kentucky Fried Chicken, they
could not start their trip until five o'clock in the afternoon. Tony
had maps and a guidebook ready, and Yun prepared some
snacks. They were as excited as two little children when his
truck finally got on the highway. Before dark, their truck safely
arrived at a beautiful house on the slope of a hill.

"This is my friend's house. He used to be a primary school
teacher, but now he's a businessman. Since he often goes on er-
rands, he asked me to check the empty house from time to time."
True, this house must be owned by a businessman. Yun did not
believe a professor could afford to buy it. The house was like a
model on display in a Washington museum. Nature was captured right in the house. On one side you could see a gentle wa-
terfall, in the center a botanical garden, a tree shooting up from
the transparent sun roof. There were no modern stairs in the
house. One had to climb a ladder to get to the second floor. When
Yun climbed up with keen curiosity, she saw a study with books
and magazines, a storeroom with hunting guns and sports
equipment, and a sleeping room with a king-size bed. Closets,
like kids playing hide-and-seek, were hard for Yun to detect
here and there.

Yun climbed down with Tony.

"This man seems to have no family."

"Right. After his girlfriend died a year ago, he has been living alone."

"What a beautiful house. I've never seen one with such aesthetic taste before."

"This is an experimental design by an architect."

Yun and Tony chatted pleasantly over coffee and a simple dinner. Then everything was quiet, almost too quiet, as if they were camping in the deep woods. But they had the comforts of civilization. While Tony was reading the newspaper, Yun fumbled with her stiff fingers over the keys of a grand piano. She did not really play, but the random music sounded beautiful. Perhaps any noise would be beautiful in such an environment. Then Tony and Yun watched TV for a long time. Tony lay in a recliner while Yun sat on a sofa. There was no awareness of sexual tension between them. The night had a lyrical taste.

After each took a shower, they realized they needed to sleep. There was only one bed in the house. Yun said she would just sleep in the sitting room. Tony smiled: "We can share the bed. The bed is huge, big enough for each of us to occupy a side."

Yun was sleeping in her high fashion dress on one side of the bed—she had bought that beautiful dress for five dollars on sale; it was too fashionable to wear for work but quite comfortable for sleep. Tony was sleeping on the other side. Their backs faced each other. One could never lie on one's side for too long, and Yun turned her body. Tony immediately turned his body and stretched an arm around her. She was silent and motionless. Tony stripped off her dress and carried her two legs on his shoulders. Yun could see in the dark that her body had been transformed into a valley. His penetration was vigorous and had good rhythm. Yun could not help making, like those female singers of pop music, sexual utterances of pain and joy. Nevertheless, there was no true orgasm, merely an unconscious simulation. The masculine poundings were becoming too heavy and mechanical and Yun had to give him hints to stop.

When he was lying down by her side as if nothing had happened, Yun asked: "You did not discharge, did you?"

"No. I am not ready to be a father yet."

"How could it stay so hard for that long?" Her husband generally held his no more than one minute and her lovers held on longer but never to the point where it became unbearable.

"I practiced."

"How did you practice?"

"By reading books and having girlfriends."

"Have you had a lot of girlfriends?"

"Yes. When I was in the service in Germany, I waited on any girl on my knees, but now I do not. I don't have a girlfriend at the moment, although girls are always interested in me."

"Don't you know I am ten years older than you?"

"Age is not a problem. But I feel a bit uneasy because you are my teacher and you have a husband." Americans were not amoral in love.

"Of course, we are not going to continue this relationship."

They slept soundly till daybreak. Before exchanging a word, they made love again. Yun did not feel great pleasure. The pounding was too vigorous. By now she knew she enjoyed the subtlety and sensitivity of the tongue and fingers much more than the real masculine weapon. They did not kiss each other. Yun could make love more easily than kissing. She shunned kissing unless a person could truly produce a reciprocal passion in her.

They had a wonderful time in New York. A few days later, he went to Beijing for further Chinese study. A year passed, and Yun's memory of him faded. One day, the department secretary told her that a young man had been looking for her.

"Is he Chinese?"

"No, an American. He waited for a long time. Then he put something in your mailbox and left."

Yun unfolded the little packet and saw that it contained a tape of Luo Dayou's songs entitled "Comrade and Love," with a few handwritten words: Love, from Tony. There was no address or telephone number.

When Yun's body was set free from the prison of love, her mind became more open and larger and her behavior became less conventional. She was living with a divorced woman in the Physics department. When they were bored during the weekend, they would invite single male graduate students to come dance in their spacious sitting room. It was sheer beauty and joy for Yun. She was glad men were always eager to be invited. The young men around her stopped playing cards and borrowed books on social dance from the library. Yun was told they practiced with each other and argued about the accuracy of each movement like a problem in math. Their appearances also showed obvious improvement—a newly acquired taste for elegance. Some men came with their young girlfriends. Those young girls, however, were too shy to dance freely and gracefully like Yun and her roommate. One weekend they danced to the boombox. Another week, Yun's idea was to have each person bring a walkman. They danced like a hurricane, as the music each soul heard was intimate and loud to him/herself and the dimly lit sitting room swirled with drunken shadows. The most enjoyable part was their talk. Young men and young girls were anxious to hear Yun's philosophy on love. She was usually sitting high in the only armchair and all the listeners sprawled on the floor in a half circle. It was like a Milky Way of stars facing the moon.

Yun became famous among the Chinese on campus. People gossiped about her and the salon in her apartment. Yun liked the term "salon" because in Chinese it meant the Sandy Dragon. She could imagine that the roomful of people danced like a dragon, with their bodies each resembling a grain of sand, undulating fluidly. Many graduate students phoned, wanting to come to her dancing party. Some of the boys started to visit her, willing to serve her in any manner they could. A young student in the Finance Department phoned her many times and said he was sick. Yun knew he meant he was lovesick. A married man suggested that they go to a movie. A sad graduate student who had been abandoned by his wife when she came to America ahead of him wanted to talk with Yun in the woods. Naturally, there was nasty gossip about her, particularly among the women. Well, what could they gossip about, if not calling her a "Yu Lejin" or something like a whore?[3] Yun had never been bothered by these prejudices. Nevertheless, she stopped because she was warned that one of the group was actually a spy from the Chinese Embassy. Yun was a practical woman and knew what the consequences would be once she went back to China. Yu Lejin had sought asylum in Germany.

Although Yun was a fascinating devil among the Chinese, she had a very innocent facade in her own department. Being a good scholar, Yun benefited not only from ancient Chinese philosophies but also from small sayings of wisdom. For instance, "A hare never eats the grass around her hole." What does it mean? Does the grass imply some material interest? No. As far as love affairs are concerned, it means that you do not get involved with anybody in your workplace. The purpose of the grass is protection. Oh, I see. That's why you are "the last puritan" in the department. Beyond the hole, a hare can graze freely.

But Yun's little philosophy of life was always smarter by half. For instance, when she became a believer in the separation of sex and love, she did not expect to be tripped up so soon.

---

[3] Yu Lejin is a pioneering contemporary woman writer who boldly handles sex and sexual politics in her writing. She is rumored to have a free lifestyle and to have organized salons.

=
5
=

Life was damned funny. No matter how smart Yun was, she never felt she could walk properly in America without a linguistic crutch. Herein is the thread of her never-intended-to-be-serious but turned all-too-genuine romance with Prues.

Yun had started learning English when she was already twenty-two years old. A certain closure in her brain refused to allow her to perfect her skill in a foreign tongue. When she wrote she needed to have papers proofread by native speakers. This incompleteness had given her a larger exposure to romance. Her proofreaders were usually males, since women seemed too preoccupied with their own studies. (She was not aware of her prejudice against women; she had seldom asked for help from her own sex.)

When Yun finished her paper on a utopian topic, she asked her classmate Prues to edit it for her. He seemed to be a nice, patient man. Three days later, he returned Yun's paper spotted with coffee and smelling of tobacco. Yet Yun was happy because his editing was good. Almost anything that feels good is a sign of romance.

Now everything becomes antique. One can even talk about Yun and Prues as if they merely existed in a silly fairy tale.

When they first met, Yun hardly noticed him. No trace of Prince Charming here. Actually there was a kind of dumbness, heaviness, slowness in Prues that Yun never disliked if those qualities had nothing to do with her.

It was purely for business reasons that Yun had cooked diligently for him, and soon her table was covered with the colors and shapes of Chinese delicacies. He phoned, unable to come on time. Bored, Yun took an evening nap. He finally came around nine o'clock. They had a delightful dinner. At about ten, Prues said he must be leaving because he was a married man. Yun replied, I am a married woman, with a daughter, too.

That was that. Yun never expected Prues to call her the following day and ask to see her. Why not? Come tomorrow at one in the afternoon.

He came. He smoked silently. Yun felt a bit strange. Finally he asked her if she'd like to take a walk in the woods. Yun put on her running shoes, ready to go. He drove into a dead end in the woods, a clearing about two rooms wide. They stood there, staring into a shaft of sky over the clearing surrounded by tall trees. Stepping over to Yun, Prues put a hand on her shoulder. She did not shake it off but walked slowly with him. He looked a contemplative man of few words. His sincere manner and honest face seemed to have commanded Yun's movements. She just followed as if under a spell. He turned solemnly to face Yun and drew her close to him and kissed her on the lips. She did not resist. She was not even thinking. Then they drove back to her apartment.

"Can we make love?"

"What?"

"Will you make love with me?   We can go to a hotel."

"Why a hotel?"

Yun went to her bedroom and he followed.

The love they had that afternoon was tasteful to Yun.   His strokes were maternal, his touch was sensitive, his penetrating had a climax as well as slow lulls.   He kissed toothlessly around her neck, shoulders, and everywhere. Yun did not sense any sexual menace or any stirs of passion. As if drowning in the sea, she was drowsy and helpless. It was pleasant, pleasant, pleasant. . . . She knew it was not the end of their affair. It would continue.

That night Yun had a sensual dream and she captured its shadow.

To Prues

An image or an impression
*   forms on the foams of*
*   a twilight consciousness*
*   smiles echo the smiles*
*   I am so intimate with.*
I struggle to wake up from a sweet dizziness
*   I see you*
*   rising from the voluptuous clouds*

The wind touches waves gently
*   They share with me the tenderness*

> *of lipped fingers*
> *The wind woos a crescendo p. . . p. . . p. . .*
> *The waves rue--rue--rue--*
> *so much pain in the fading pleasure*
> *S . . . s . . . s . . .*
> *The tired tire sighs*
> *in a timely puncture*

> *Needles of love sieve over*
> *yellow petals of Welcome Spring*
> *So deep*
> *piercing into invisible cells*
> *ramificating*
> *reaching the nerves of loins*
> *A Beatific Shudder*

> *I hold my Waterbaby tighter*
> *feeling a nine-month child*
> *wriggling in the Womb of Nature*
> *watching a thrust of passion*
> *through wide-open pores*
> *spray beads of wetness*
> *into the misty air*

> *I dwindle with you into*
> *an Eros in birthday suit*
> *gently brushed by the sensitivity of poetry*
> *quivering, its fingertips*
> *tantalizing me in coziness*
> *paralyzing me*

> *I say*
> *I know why a Fool loves to drown*
> *in the sea —*
> *Love, my archenemy.*

Yun did not mind having an affair with Prues, but she resisted love. She defined her relationship with him as a diversification of life. After all, Prues was not mute. He started to talk and his little talks were always honest and funny. He told her he had married Karen at the age of eighteen simply because she liked to wear tight pants and was very sexy. Then he grumbled that he had been cheated into marriage because Karen gave a false alarm about her pregnancy. Well, he and Karen had separated for eight years and gotten back together a couple of years ago. Karen had been a terrible spender in their early married life. No matter how much Prues earned, he could not catch up with her expenses.

"I was an assistant pilot in the Air Force then. When I was away on a mission I did not spend money in restaurants but lived on cheap crackers. When I got home, I found Karen had again abused my credit card, leaving me two thousand dollars in debt."

"How did she do it?"

" Well, one can easily buy a lot of things from a store and then send them back for a refund."

"I see. Why did she need that much money? To buy clothes?"

"I really don't know. Once I came home and walked in the front door, while her lover stole out the back."

"So one day, I just drove away. Eight years later when I met her, she was completely reformed. After I abandoned her, she worked hard to raise our two kids. She even paid her way through vocational college and got a diploma as an X-ray technician. . . ."

Yun had a pretty good impression of Karen. She was not stealing Prues away from her but wanted to make them happier.

It was quite true that Prues had changed into a better man after meeting Yun. He became cheerful, diligent, and considerate at home. He became more innovative in their marital relationship. During the spring break, he took Karen to a cabin on the beach for romance.

Karen was a reflection of his happiness. One day Prues said, "Karen is beaming with sweetness these days; perhaps she has a lover in her school. I want to follow her this afternoon."

"If this is true, then you have become equals. Why do you need to follow her?"

" Well, just for fun."

When a man is following his wife, it is not for fun. Yun knew a handsome, intelligent man who had been abandoned by her wife because he followed her into the woods with a man. A woman of dignity certainly cannot live with such humiliation.

Prues never mentioned his feelings towards Yun, except to make a passing comment like "You have a good pussy." If Prues had not candidly confessed that he dreamed of women 90% of the time, she would have felt insulted. "I simply cannot concentrate on anything. If I am reading, I am fantasizing in the back of my mind."

A man of Prues' level could hardly make Yun cling to him. As they parted each time, she instantly turned to her study.

One day Prues popped into her office.

"What a nice spring day! Let's go to the woods."

"I want to finish reading this book."

"Come on. Take it to read in the woods." He dragged her out of her cubicle.

He drove into a dense bush and wanted to make love. Yun was having her period and it was considered a sin in Chinese culture to make love during that period.

"Never mind. American women feel more horny during that period." Perhaps this was true for all women.

They made love in nature for the first time. The beach towel was dyed red.

"I had a sexual fantasy dream when I woke up this morning. I kept thinking of you and simply couldn't get over it." Prues was satisfied.

A week later Yun told Prues that her husband and child were arriving in New York and asked him to pick them up from the airport with her. She felt happy and excited over Long and Mei's coming and hated herself for being unable to turn into a roc and carry Mei back from Kennedy Airport on her giant wings. But she did not expect Prues to become ghastly pale. He stammered that he could not let Yun leave him. "I am not leaving you. You have your wife and children around you and I have mine. Now we are perfectly equal," Yun said with ease.

There was a change in Prues. He threw himself into pathos and mumbled about his splitting love between Yun and Karen. Yun simply told him to stop his foolish indulgence, as she saw no conflict between her and Karen. One day he declared he wanted to marry Yun. "Madman. Do you want to be called Prues Hu?" Yun teased him. He nodded quite seriously.

The following evening Yun received a call while having dinner with her family.

"Who is this? Karen, Prues's wife?"

"Yes. We must have a talk at Pizza Hut."

"Okay, take Prues with you."

Karen was not mad at her. She actually said that she knew about Yun's relationship with Prues and she did not want to be left out. "Join us then. We three can enjoy some pleasant time together," Yun said candidly. Karen even suggested renting a large house so that Yun's family and her family could live harmoniously together in a utopian manner. Perhaps it was possible. Yun had seen a movie about communal love.

After their conference:
"How could you tell your wife about our relationship? Now you won't have a moment of peace."
" Well, last night Karen and I pledged to each other our mutual honesty in everything. So I told her about you."
Karen kept phoning Yun and telling her how she loved Prues. Yun understood and said she had no intention of taking Prues away from her and promised not even to have sex with him anymore.

For quite a few days Yun tried not to go anywhere with Prues. One day, when Yun was feeling miserable with a backache, Prues came to see her in her office and suggested going to a spa. She had seen a poster for a spa that had included a photo of a group of youngsters. Perhaps the spa was a pond of hot spring water. She went along with him. Well, the spa turned out to be completely different from what she'd expected. It was enclosed in a private room. They played alone like fish in a huge tub. The rushing water aroused their desire and they made love.

It was truly relaxing. The pain in Yun's back was gone. But that evening Karen called her.
"Can you believe that Prues made love with a woman named Vivien in the town spa? I happen to have a friend who works there. She phoned me and I went over and found their used con-dom." Yun knew she had been following them.
" Well, I was that woman." She hung up the phone.

Prues was barred from his home. He broke the window the next day, smuggled his own belongings out, and went to rent a room. Prues actually looked quite cheerful. He was liberated. He felt free again like a new baby. He immediately invited Yun to visit his realm of independence. It was a new house. Because of its out-of-the-way location, the rent was cheap. His house-mates were bums, lazy people seeking the essence of life. They looked all like amateur artists and were vegetarians. Prues started a diet of greens and rice. He lost some weight and looked taller. When Yun went over, he cooked for her and they made love three times in an hour.
"Do you really want to marry me?"
"I am not sure. You might be a worse tyrant than Karen."
"You are right."
A few days passed. Karen phoned Yun again.

"Can you believe that my daughter saw Prues holding Jacklin in his arms at the Best Cafe? I am pretty sure he is having an affair with her."

" Well, you let him go," Yun said in good humor.

Yun felt bad about Prues anyway. She asked him whether it was true. It was true.

"My daughter called me an asshole; she could not understand my longing to reach out to different women. The more I stretch out the keener I feel my love for you. I told Jacklin when we were having sex how I love you."

" Well, goodbye." Yun grabbed a pen and smudged a card she had given him.

> *Goodbye*
> *A short-lived past*
> *dispersing darkness*
> *from the Icehole*
> *of Father Night.*

A theory is good as long as you are not the victim of it. When it comes to the real test, Yun could not share love, just like Karen.

The next day when Prues passed by Yun, she refused to speak to him.

At home, Yun's husband had finally decided to get a divorce because of her relationship with Prues. It sounded like a crisis. But Yun felt indifferent. She and Long went to the County offices and filled out the divorce papers. She went to Chicago for a conference. When she came back, Long surprisingly pleaded with her not to file the papers. He was sorry that he was unable to please her as Prues had and suggested that she go on with Prues. As long as they did not have to divorce, everything was okay with him. "I should have been more tolerant," he said. Stranger than this, Karen had called Yun and begged her to continue her relationship with Prues, even if it meant his having an affair. Karen had Prues back from his realm of independence but had no heart to see him suffer.

Yun felt damned funny about Long and Karen, but she also was touched by their love and care. When Yun and Prues got back together, Prues forgot both Jacklin and Karen. Karen had refused to speak to Jacklin when they met in church; now they were reconciled. Jacklin simply faded out of Prues's picture. But Karen could not.

Yun did not make love with Prues anymore but met him regularly in the evening for summer chats. Prues was writing a science fiction novel and was deeply involved in his work.

Another two weeks passed. Saturday, while Yun was preparing for her doctoral exams, Karen came. *Dear me, she must have lost thirty pounds at least.* Her face had narrowed an inch and her eyes were scorched by excessive tears.

Yun felt a deep sympathy for her.

"Tell me, Karen. What's the problem?"

Karen told Yun how she loved Prues and could not bear a separation from him, not even emotionally. Her tears fell mutely. Yun understood her.

"I am not taking Prues away from you. I do not wish to marry him. Karen, a woman must have a center in herself. If he does not love you as deeply as you love him, he is not worth your suffering. Why don't you also reach out to other men?

"Can't you see that Prues has become a better man for you? He has stopped drinking and smoking. He writes day and night. In fact, except for literary subjects, nowadays we hardly talk about anything."

Karen dried her tears and said she was going to apply to the master's program in education.

She began to come to Prues's office with him. He revised her papers as he had for Yun. Karen's face brightened up.

After her sixteen hours of comprehensive exams, Prues invited Yun to see the videotape *Lolita* at his buddy's apartment. During the movie, Prues kissed her neck and shoulders. Yun collapsed under the voluptuous seduction of the sea. Suddenly Prues tunneled under the white sheet covering her body like a badger. He kissed her underlips and made violent love with his tongue. Yun became nearly hysterical and begged him to stop. But he penetrated her with even more eagerness. Yun screamed and felt paralyzed. Perhaps it was an orgasm, the only one she had ever had in her life.

She was exhausted and left him without a word. For the first time she desired to cling to somebody or something for life before death.

> *A green leaf*
>   *drifting on the open sea*
> *how she yearns to cling*
>   *cling to a twig*
>   *to a splint of wood*

to a ship
she knows her independence breathes
in floating
alone
Yet such a desire to cling
before she turns yellow
brown
vanishing in the death of gray.

When they met again, Prues apologized for his animal behavior. Yun told him she had enjoyed it. He embraced her tightly and murmured his love. His whole body was trembling like
a little animal, with such tragic intensity. Prues was not a poet
but lived a poem. Yun held him desperately as if this poetic vision would fade away.

Twenty
fingernails dug deep
into our intertwined trunks
which are melting
shaping the fair Hermaphrodite
yours smells me
mine tastes you
There is no more she, there is no more he
Suddenly butcher words cut us
asunder
Between two bleeding halves
such a divine loss
No space and time
can
ever make up.

"I accepted a semester appointment at Duke University."
On hearing Yun's news, he must have felt like death.

They had a last dinner together. No, it was not dinner, but
a brunch at Elby's.
"I have a little dream in my life."
"What's that?"
"One is always the complement of the other. My ideal
man is my proofreader. If he reads my writing for two hours, I
will do two hours of service for him in an area he dislikes or is

unable to perform in."

" You seem to demand very little."

" Yes. We'll study, talk, and visit Paris and Rome together if we can afford to. If not, we still can wander in the wild woods or stroll around the courtyard. We jump like elves when we are happy. At the moments of sadness, we hold each other tightly like a crying baby in the arms of its heartbroken mother . . . ."

From Elby's, they drove to a quiet place in the small car Prues had just bought. Standing on the bridge, Yun could smell alcohol on Prues and he was smoking a cigarette.

"Oh, Prues—"

"What?"

"I had only one purpose today: to make love with you. Life has denied me. I want you, like many women who dare take men as sexual objects."

"I should never have sold my big old car." Yun and Prues had made love in that car in the woods.

"This is the first time that I have declared my desire for a man's body, isn't it?"

" Yes, you must have been terribly starved."

"No, it's only another frame of my mind. I feel the impulse to declare my vulgar desires."

"I like you because you behave like a man in many aspects. We can talk like buddies."

"Never mind. I can transfer my desire for you to Long tonight . . . ."

"Please, don't. After all my efforts to work you up. We should go to a motel tonight."

She neither said yes nor objected. Her mind was re-feeling how she felt outside the car, treading on the dead leaves by the stream a moment ago.

It seems that a woman's feeling has to be hung somewhere
Then let mine silver the distant white clouds
when I separate from man's wine evaporation
walking out of his smoking mist
Oh, how bright the sun shines
stroking the tender fibers of my heart
flirting with my blinking eyes
My vision, like waves of magnet or radiation,
expands beyond the finite
horizon.

While Prues was asking Yun about the rain forests in China, she was absentmindedly daydreaming.

"Why are you smiling? About the word 'virgin'?"

"What?"

" You just said China still has some virgin forests."

"Did I?"

"I'll be in my office at eight tonight."

She knew she was not going.

=
6
=

When Yun flew back from Durham for her dissertation defense, she invited both Prues and Karen to the Peking Garden for dinner. They chatted like old buddies. Prues seemed to be too preoccupied to pay much attention to Yun. When he drove her to the airport, she noticed that he looked like an old farmer, with dirt and thorny seeds all over his shirt.

"How come you look like this?"

"I've been working in the woods these two days."

"Why?"

" Well, I planted some pops there in the spring. Quite unexpectedly, I've got a good harvest."

"Pops? A kind of vegetable for cooking?"

"No. It's one of the mildest drugs."

"Drugs? That's illegal, isn't it?"

" Yes. It was forbidden by the law some years ago. But don't be alarmed; I know some professors who take it. A little is not that harmful and it's good for the imagination."

"Are you thinking of Edgar Allen Poe? Why did you do this?" Yun felt threatened by his criminal activity.

" You know the American dream. In this world, the value of drugs equals gold. A small bag of drugs will make you rich."

"I never want to be rich through devious activities."

"If I did not grow it, someone would have to smuggle it from abroad. For drug addicts, it makes no difference."

"Still, I do not want you to be caught by the police before you get rich."

"Don't worry. I plan to do it for two years. Then I will have enough money for a meager, leisurely existence. I would read books like Thoreau in a cabin and write my novels and plays. . . ."

A noble intention, a criminal act.

"How could you quit teaching composition during the spring semester? Did you discuss it with Karen?"

"Yes. I did. You may think it's foolish, but I need more time for writing and spring is the time for sowing."

"I hope you stop before it is too late. It is not worth taking that risk."

Five days later Yun got a letter from Prues. He had finished harvesting and was ready to get back to his reading and writing. And he had decided not to grow anything in the woods any more.

The following night, Karen called Yun.

"Did you hear that Prues was arrested?"

"Arrested? For what?"

"For pops."

"What pops? He drank too much beer before driving?" Perhaps every human being has an instinct for self-protection.

"No. Pops is a kind of drug."

"He's taking drugs again?"

"No, he grew some pops in the woods."

"Did you know this?"

"How could I know?"

"I'm sorry to hear this. I will visit him in jail when I get back to Pitt next month."

When Yun returned, she phoned Karen and learned that Prues had been bailed out by his good friends among the graduate students and professors. Prues was a good man, and Karen said that Prues had became an even better man. He confessed all his sins to her during her visit to the jail. Yun knew it was his last judgment day. Karen had pardoned him as God would and loved him even more.

The following day when Prues came to see Yun, he looked thinner. His pale, calm appearance indicated that every cell in his body had been cleansed. They drove to a stream in the woods. He talked about the books he had been reading lately, Freud, Jung, Kafka. . . . He said he had a strong interest in feminism, too.

"What have you planned for your life?"

"Nothing. I am sick of the world. I just want to stay at home reading. Of course I cook daily for the family."

"Karen is the sole breadwinner then."

"Yes, but she is happy. She would rather have me at home all the time than dissipating outside."

Prues had been ennobled and womanized at once.

Yun soon moved with her family to Los Angeles. Now she entered her second year at the University of Southern California. Prues and Karen were stored in her memory. She sometimes retrieved their file to reflect upon herself. She knew that she would die rather than take a man from a woman. Her love and sympathy for women were, most of the time, stronger than for men.

One day Yun received a letter from Prues. He had separated from Karen because of her fits of anger and because she watched TV all the time and acted as though he did not exist. Prues was supporting himself by editing for students on campus. A meager living, indeed, but he was happier. He had found that his talent was writing screenplays and wished to come to Los Angeles to meet celebrities in the field. Yun knew that his dream was an illusion. No celebrities would even want to look at him. The screenplay he had submitted to UCLA for a contest had probably been dropped into a wastebasket. She did not want to hurt him with the truth. Instead, she wrote him a letter encouraging him to go on with his writing but not to be concerned with celebrities or contests. Writing is the best means of self-exploration. A month later Prues called Yun, saying he felt no hope in his life and wanted to come to her in Los Angeles. Yun was tempted by his offer. She was in dire need of an editor for her book and her relationship with Long was the worst it had ever been. Once, she had asked something while Long was chopping cabbage. He had raised the big Chinese knife in his hand and roared. Yun was leaving for an appointment at Cal Poly. She was a new driver and Cal Poly then was a new place. She felt nervous on high-ways, particularly to a strange place. Long chased her to the door and said with clenched teeth: I hope you die under the wheels today. When she got on the freeway, her whole body was shaking. She pinched her thigh fiercely until blood came out. She calmed down and arrived safely. However, it was immoral to take advantage of the crisis between Prues and Karen. Karen had loved him under all circumstances and Prues loved her more than he recognized. So Yun wrote her last letter to him.

> *Dear Prues:*
>   *It is the first time that you have said that you feel there is no hope in your life. You will see hope when you turn your eyes in a different direction. After you were convicted, you changed into a coward. You hid yourself in the kitchen and used pompous theories to disguise your emptiness. You are always complaining about Karen's faults and wished her to be a feminist, a thinking woman like me. But do you realize that she is a*

*feminist? When you first abandoned her she found
herself a job and raised two children; the second time
you left home, she found herself a permanent job with
better pay. You told me this, didn't you?*

*When she showers you with fits of anger or watches
TV in a sullen mood, she is protesting against your
cowardice. A man should never give up his manhood.
A woman cannot be satisfied with an angel in the
house.*

*Please talk with Karen. I love you and Karen
equally, but with a shred more admiration for her. Do
you remember how thin she became for love of you that
summer? She has never abandoned the man she has
loved since childhood.*

*Be brave in life and go back to her. I wish you all
the happiness in the world.*

*My relationship with Long has improved lately.
We've separated our money. Let him feel his independence at home. Yes, I am still suffering. But if it is the
bitter fruit of my domestic domination, I have to either
change or bear it.*

Love,

Yun

Ten days later when Yun came home from school, Mei told
her that Karen had called her.

"How do you know it was Karen? Did she leave her name or
phone number?"

"Of course I know her voice. She used to call us like a crazy
woman at Pittsburgh. She said she would like to talk to you, but
left no number. Perhaps she will call back."

Yun knew she would not call back. Yun expected no gratitude or blame. Prues and Karen definitely got back together.
There was no guarantee that they would not split up again. But it
was time for Yun to vanish permanently from their life.
Perhaps Karen was right. Yun was merely a big flirt. Being too
self-centered, moralistic, and self-scrutinizing, in real life she
would not marry anyone else, and she had to wear out her marital jail.

God's Punishment

In the spousal cellar,
 the stallions of my
  innerness
   are frozen onto
    a   relief on the wall.

A Separate Utopia

Seven months have passed since I said goodbye to Ramon. I do not see men anymore. People all appear exceptionally friendly to me. "Hi, Hu." "Hi, Yun." "Hi—". . . *Seeing is no-seeing just as before.* Now it is January 1993. Los Angeles County has been flooded, persistent rain sliding chunks of earth toward those vulnerable houses, swooping them up like little chicks.

What I have been doing these days? Defecating. True, my bedroom or my studio is exactly like the public bathroom I once saw on another planet—the utopia of plagiarism, I would call it. A large master room with a queen-sized bed, an extraordinarily long desk, computer, printer, typewriter, file cabinet, nine-drawer dresser, and large vanity. Look at the books, stacked by the desk, sprawling on the floor, hiding under the bed. The recent favorites are like concubines lying on my bed. I am not a faithful queen, changing my concubines quicker than the female Emperor Wu Zetian. Everywhere in my room you can reach for note pads, scratch paper, dark pencils, blue pens, red markers. Mine is a forbidden city into which my husband cannot peer without permission. But my daughter is always curious; she snickers behind me from time to time, watching me defecate. "Stop that, Mei. Can you respect my privacy? When I have finished, I'll show you." Right, it is largely for her I have taken larger dozes of laxative than the doctor prescribed to speed up my defecation. Did my guide, the alien, say, one man's excrement is another's food?

Yesterday it was raining harder than ever before. I heard rumbling thunder. Today, the news reported that one man had been struck dead by lightning. I feel very guilty, because the lightning had been for me—an unfilial daughter. Last night my father's apparition, the God of Thunder with two huge round hammers in his hands, came to visit me. His tiger fangs were sticking out five inches. Flapping over my bird droppings on several white sheets, he flew into a rage.

"How dare you portray me as a tyrant! Without me, could the Chinese have been free from Japanese devils and other foreign monsters? Without me, could the Chinese have a good life today? Without me opening the door first for you with the ping pong policy, how could you come to America? Without me, could you ever have been born?"

He clashed his two hammers angrily and left—"Watch my lightning tomorrow!"

I was not scared because I still remembered the late Mao Zedong's quotation by heart, "Fear no death nor hardship." Strange indeed, the God of Thunder was first my father but when he was parting he changed to Chairman Mao. I knew I was going to be struck dead by lightning the next day because in one of my caricatures done thirty years ago, at the age of twelve, I sketched Mao as a woman with two pigtails. Although I had been crammed since my childhood with abstract terms such as socialism, capitalism, imperialism, Marxism, Leninism, Stalinism, Maoism, I could not make much sense of them. But when I saw the huge portraits of Ma-En-Lie-Si-Mao[1] hanging on the wall of the City Hall, I could not help noticing the progressive shortening of the beards until I reached the beardless portrait of Mao.

The rain poured dark ink on the night. I looked from my window and saw the whole sky become a bankless river. More strangely, the parting Mao, dwindling smaller but more stout, transfigured into Deng Xiaoping. No mistake, I could see two pets running by his side: a black cat and a white cat. It is said he feeds an extra fish daily to the cat who has caught a mouse. "Be careful!" I shouted to him, forgetting my fear, when I saw he was wading through the flood like a child twaddling on river stones. He laughed over his shoulder, "Lady Idiot, don't you know I am demonstrating my current policy of modernizing China by grasping stones in the river, which is much more reliable than the policy of 'jumping a chasm' in Eastern Europe. *With me in power, be at ease.*"

"You are plagiarizing Mao's quotation for Hua Guofeng." Fortunately Deng disappeared before he heard my mumbling.

I must have been born a bold lover. Although I rebelled against my father for his tyranny, I was sexually attracted to him, perhaps at the age of sixteen. One day he cornered me in a

---

[1] Marx, Engels, Lenin, Stalin, and Mao.

room and hugged me. I struggled away from him. But after that he looked at me with a softer eye. The day I left home for re-education in the countryside, he bought me a red, round apple the size of a baby's head. Once I left home, I never went back. I know my parents love better my other sisters and brothers, who surround them like satellites, buying coal and grain for them, taking them to the hospital, and sharing their festival meals. But whenever my father talked with his colleagues he would mention my name, the one who has been to Britain and now is in America.

The day before I left for America, all my relatives came to say goodbye. At the farewell dinner party, the seven grand-children, each an only child and the lord of a nuclear family, created great havoc like the seven warring states in ancient China. My nephew threw a large piece of meat across the table at his "enemy" while my niece, a five-year-old, was sowing cooked rice all over the floor. My mother looked at their young mothers and said, "Spare the rod and spoil the child." My elder brother raised his hand at his son, but the urchin laughed at him, "Don't put up a show, Papa."

Someone knocked at the door. My mother opened the door and saw it was a beggar. She went to the kitchen and fetched a large bowl of rice and meat. But two big grandchildren stopped my mother on her way to the door with their toy guns and shouted: "Don't feed those beggars; they are just too lazy to earn a living." The beggar stuck a piece of paper on our door and left. A verse was written on the paper.

The Family Tree

A split in the stem
Of a fruitful bloom,
Yellow siblings have brought the doom.
Scattering themselves in their own gloom,
No more connections to the root.
Falling apart, a cracking crown,
No more quarreling around a withering frown.
Unity flees from a torn family gown,
A line by its splattered abundance weighed down.

After I read it to my mother, she became ghastly pale. I took out ten *yuan* from my wallet and was about to get the beggar back to write a poem of good luck for us. My mother waved her hand

and murmured, "Too late. It's our fate."

My father was blind to all these happenings, as a grandson was riding on his back with two chubby hands around his neck and a granddaughter, sitting on his lap, was rebuttoning his Maoist uniform in a new order. When I asked my father to tell his past to those spoiled children, he shook his head in silence. Ever since 1966 when he was criticized and labeled a Communist renegade and a capitalist traveler, he had stopped talking about his glorious past. However, he wrote me three letters before his death. Each of them told me of his visits to places he had fought in as a soldier during his heroic days. I wrote to ask him to write a memoir and I even sent him a tape-recorder for this purpose. But he died like a bolt from the blue. Long heard that before my father had his heart attack he was angered by a quarrel about the baby chickens with our neighbor, a retired cadre and a brave soldier like him. Should a great man have died over such a trivial thing?

My elder sister said that she took an express train to Nanyang that day (why so quickly, if you were not thinking about getting a share of his property?) and found out that our father left no money at all. Everybody was disappointed; fighting for socialism over the last forty years had earned nothing, absolutely nothing. Who is going to take care of our aged mother, now deaf? The state only gives her forty *yuan* pension a month, not quite enough to buy toilet paper in America. All right, each of you six children will give her twenty *yuan* a month, and I will mail her two hundred dollars a year. Great, the more children the more secure one feels in old age. I understand why it is so hard for women to have their tubes tied.

Did I send a check to China this year? Yes, I did it two weeks ago. I hope my mother will get it before the Chinese New Year.

I dare to not only love my father as a woman would but also love the greatest leaders of the nation. I loved Mao Zedong and Deng Xiaoping passionately. Even though Mao passed away a dozen years ago, my passion for him refuses to surrender. I still feel bitterness and jealousy when I see him, in my mind, surrounded by sexless women, one of them holding a hammer, one holding a rifle, one holding a bundle of wheat, one holding his Little Red Book. . . all of them have one hand raised up in the pose of the Liberty Statue. Oh, I see. They are holding half of the sky. I tried very hard to follow Mao's instructions but was never able to catch up with other women. The day I left the countryside for Britain, I stood by my experimental plot, seeing the wheat withered into dry weed, and cried like an unrequited lover. In London, when Chinese students heard the news of his death, we left school and wept in our bedrooms. Others did it, perhaps, for different reasons. I did so purely for love. I disliked his poem that says women should like guns, not feminine attire; but I loved his feminine sentiments, "I lost my Poplar; you your Willow. . . ." I have learned, from the *People's Daily*, that the Chinese are building a six-meter bronze statue of Mao Zedong in his hometown, Shaoshan. I cried for him because as his secret lover, I know he would prefer to have his body whipped rather than worshiped without flesh and spirit. I loathe his big talks but like his small sayings, such as "A person must have some spirit." Now I wonder whether the gold apples in Jinzhou can grow fast enough to feed the worms nestling in the Great Wall.[2]

Why do I love Deng Xiaoping? First, Mao is dead. As pragmatic as any other Chinese woman, I have switched my love to fit the historical tide. I used to be a Romanticist and believe first things never die: first smile, first sight, first sound. My experience with Deng Xiaoping is entirely different. I loathed him as a man; he was a bit short and he seemed to grit his teeth even when he was smiling. I never heard his voice but I could well imagine that a musical sound would not come from such a stumpy body. He looked macho, too masculine for my taste. Moreover, before I got to cultivate nice feelings about him, I heard rumors such as a student had committed suicide by jumping from a ten-story building because Deng Xiaoping had pulled down the Democratic Wall. Loathing to see his face, I refused to read any Chinese newspapers for at least half a year. During the June 4th incident, I saw on the TV news that blood had been shed on Tian An Men Square; I felt my hatred for him reaching zenith. But the intensive hatred might disguise or breed love. As the old Chinese saying goes, "A great beauty always loves a great hero." I am no beauty in others' eyes, but every woman should be a great beauty in her own eyes. So I started to pay close attention to him, reading his talks, examining his photos. By

---

[2] Jinzhou is a land of apples. When the People's Liberation Army entered it in 1948, apples were heaped along the streets and everywhere else, but no PLA solders would touch a single one. So Mao said "A person must have some spirit" to praise them. But now, according to a Chinese news report, the corrupt PLA officers in Jinzhou have sold official proof of military enrollment, Party membership, and even meritorious awards at an exorbitant price to those who never have been in service but want the privileges of a veteran.

The People's Liberation Army is known as the Great Wall.

and by his image has changed a lot. Do not laugh at me. Deng Xiaoping gradually became the very image of the extra-terrestrial in the American movie *ET*, one who cures a child's wound with his inner power and mumbles nostalgically "home, home" like an old granny.

Perhaps I am merely shaping him to become the model of my ideal lover, but I have fallen in love with him hopelessly. Lately, I have been suffering a lot from sexual jealousy. I simply cannot get rid of my nightmares. In one dream I see Deng Xiaoping is surrounded by sexy movie stars, pop singers, and fashion models. Some of them are wearing erotic nightgowns; some hardly have a thread on. Deng himself, like an emperor, is wearing a fashionable jacket, worth eight million dollars. He accidentally flips his cigarette butt and the ash falls on his jacket. His guards immediately replace his jacket with a new one, worth thirteen million dollars. His goal is to wear a thirteen hundred million dollar jacket so that he can personally feel every Chinese in the country becomes rich. My love for him is bursting, but since we are separated by the Pacific Ocean, I am afraid he will never know it.

In another dream, I see his underlings present him with a stack of documents. He orders me, his personal secretary, to read them and then report on the main ideas. Of course I report the good news first. "According to the statistics, under your wise policy of 'groping river stones,' our national economy has been increasing at the rate of 12.2% since 1983, well past the speed of the four dragonlets in Asia."[3] Deng is very pleased, casting an amorous eye at me. My heart is thrilled. "But, because I love you I have to tell you the truth—the rate of suicide has caught up with that of America, to about 400 people killing themselves daily."

"Oh, the figure is not as big as I expected. I predict that one percent of the population should be ready to be sacrificed for our four modernizations." Deng frowns.

Trying to please him, I jump over a lot of national news to report to him how his daughters and sons have been doing in the country. Although the TV series *The Elegy of the Yellow River* has been banned, we must recognize the truth in it: our civilization of the Yellow Earth is behind the civilization of the Blue Sea by 300 years at least. Consequently, the famous English Enclosure Movement has just started in China. "Two of your

---

[3] South Korea, Taiwan, Singapore and Hong Kong are known as the four dragonlets because of their "miracle economies."

children have taken the western Nanjing Road as their enclosure without spending a cent. The document says they will reap
dollars at an astronomical rate; this kind of bureaucrat-monoply capital can only occur in Red China."

"Is the last sentence your own comment?"

"No, it is printed in black and white. Please read here; it
says the Bureaucrat-monoply capital has well surpassed that of
the 'Jiang-Song-Kong-Chen'⁴ in China before 1949."

"Nonsense! Who is the author of this document?"

"A Canadian scholar."

"Absolutely unreliable."

I do not know whether he is referring to me or to the scholar.
But after Deng leaves, his guards come in to drag me into a
well—the fate of a favorite concubine at the imperial court.

I woke up in sweat, calling for help from my mother.

My mother had told me once that a leader of a nation has to
be hermaphrodite, half man and half woman, not too much a
man and not too much a woman.

How is Mother now? You are deaf, unable to hear me anymore. But I remember you, remember the night my father called
all the children up to see you. You looked as though you were
dying in a nightmare. Your eyes were staring at the ceiling.
With foam at the corners of your mouth, you shouted, "You go,
you go! No, I won't follow, I won't follow!" Later, when I asked
you what your shout meant, you smiled gently and said, "Did I
say that? I cannot remember." I know you resist the things you
do not approve of in your bones.

---

⁴ The four comprador-capitalist families.

=
2
=

I must confess that recently I have discovered myself to be a pan-sexual maniac. I can hear sexual utterances in most decent music, I can see sex in well-clothed paintings, I can feel any dance, like the modern Tango, with its whirlpool-like bed rhythm. That is why I cannot go back to China anymore. I love America as the cradle of pansexualism—sexualizing art, philosophy, literature, sociology, anthropology, mathematics, physics, war, peace, food, defecation. . . . The Chinese on the mainland are still in their infancy as far as true sex is concerned. I shut my eyes and can now see China, a female body tied with her limbs to the four corners of the earth, being pumped almost too vigorously by an extra-large Western penis. She groans with pain and with pleasure. She is simulating an orgasm.

A week ago I received a letter from my brother, a police officer. He said he had made a special trip to the open city Shenzhen to investigate Henan prostitutes in that area. He was disturbed throughout the night by about 20 phone calls from body-sellers. During the peak hours, between ten to midnight and four or five o'clock in the morning, there was absolutely no way to fall asleep. When he cross-examined a young girl from Xinxiang, the girl confessed that she had come to Shenzhen simply to follow her elder sister's model. Her sister came to Shenzhen five years ago and made forty thousand dollars by selling her body in hotels for ten months. She went back with the money and set up a business of her own. Although everybody knows her starting money is dirty, nobody minds. She now is the head of an enterprise and happily married. My brother commented that perhaps one has to do the wrong thing at the right place and right time. It was bad luck for the girl to try to emulate her sister, because the girl was not only caught but found to have AIDS.

My sister in Beijing also sent me a letter. She said that although being a university teacher is no way to get rich, the country is thriving day by day. Now we can see Russian blonds waiting on Chinese men in hotels. And a colleague, who just came back from a trip to Vietnam, says that Vietnam is in extreme poverty. Their people look up to China as a paradise. They are crazy for our *Renminbi*, just as we are crazy for U.S. dollars. Their markets contain nothing but goods made in China. Everywhere you go, you will be accosted by beautiful young Vietnamese ladies. If you can pay three hundred yuan Renminbi, you can spend a wonderful night with a lady in a high-class hotel without being disturbed by their security guards. That colleague heard a dreadful open secret that the Vietnamese are determined to sacrifice two generations of women to get their modernization started.

"Mei, are you home? Bring me the Chinese newspaper, please."

" Wait a minute. I am changing my wet clothes."

Poor girl, nobody brought her home from school in such heavy rain. I have been very sick for three weeks now.

"Are you getting better, Mom?" She took a pile of free Chinese newspapers Long picked up daily from the Hong Kong Supermarket.

"Not really. But I want to read something. How was your day today?"

"A boy kicked my cart and called me a mama's girl." I shouldn't have encouraged her to be different by using a shopping cart for her heavy books.

"Mom, is it true that the Last Judgment Day is coming this year? The Bible says it comes when a child has a baby and a man becomes pregnant. In our school, a twelve-year old girl is carrying a baby now. I read in yesterday's paper that a man is pregnant." I read about that man, too. His baby, about three pounds, was removed dead from his body because he had no womb.

"Nonsense, men have been pregnant all the time; otherwise, how can we read Shakespeare and the *Dream of the Red Chamber* today?"

"I like your jokes. But I mean real babies, not immortal babies."

My eyes catch the title of a reportage carried on November 23, 1992 *Shenzhou Times*, "The Lost Little Suns." While reading it, my heart bleeds, as if the parade of parents who lost their only sons and daughters were passing by my window. The rain is crying for them. The Chinese used to regard commerce as contemptible, but today their concepts of value have so changed that they compare the magnetic power of "trade or business" to an irresistible sea. Now everybody has plunged into the "sea" to fish for money; if you cannot sell shares in the stock market or set up a business or buy East and sell West, you can kidnap children or women. Quite a few writers are celebrating the soul of commerce. But how many have splashed their ink for the children and women whose bodies are being trampled by the iron heels of Modernization?

After scanning through the pile of papers, I feel as if my brain were congested.

"Mei, please come. I want to defecate."

"How can I help you?"

"Get some white sheets ready for what I am going to drop."

Mei puts a new paper tray by the side of my bed and withdraws quietly. A good girl, she knows a person needs privacy during defecating.

It is a privileged feeling to enjoy the freedom of defecating in bed. I remember when Mei was two months old, because I had diluted her milk with too much water, and she suffered an unspeakable constipation. I can still see her little purple face, her tightened little fists, and her stiff kicking legs.

Defecating in bed is a long journey through dreams.

"Hey, your green card." The customs officer called after me.

How could I forget to take it back? If I lost it, I would indeed become a woman without a country to live in.

Leaving the Capital Airport, I went to look for my sister in Qinghua in the Western suburbs of Beijing. It was a drizzling day. Turning to a smaller street in a residential area, I met a parading crowd holding a huge slogan that read: "Save the children!" Huh, plagiarized from Lu Xun. I felt instantly at home, with my feet planted on the land of plagiarism. The faces of the demonstrators were quite familiar to me. Right, I just read the reportage about them and their lost children. China has changed at last in the direction of democracy. Not only do journalists report the truth but people have the freedom to demonstrate for individual causes.

The following morning I got up early and visited the model of reform in heavy industry—the Capital Iron and Steel Factory. Their advanced equipment struck me as familiar. I soon learned from a manager that they shipped the entire California Iron and Steel factory here. What a capacity! Can you imagine

that the Chinese bought that black monster wholesale and hauled
it intact to China from the other shore of the Pacific Ocean? I was
told by a young worker that China was going to buy and move the
Las Vegas Casino and California Disneyland and Beverly
Hills in time so that the Chinese-earned U. S. dollars would not
be taken back by Americans.

The day I arrived in Shanghai, the street to Hongkou Park
was flanked by nine layers of people on each side. I elbowed my
way inside like a Red Guard, just in time to catch the last truck
moving slowly to an execution ground. A criminal, tied zigzag
with ropes, had a huge placard on his back that said, "Chief
Kidnapper of Children and Women." I let out a cry of relief.
Those criminals deserve to be chopped into millions of pieces.
Craning my neck to see that criminal off, I stepped on somebody's toe.

"Ouch. Ah, it's you,Yun."

She was Li Jie, the "Puritan" of my class when I studied in
Shanghai. She said her brother happened to be the guard of that
criminal and knew the case pretty well. Then she fumbled in
her briefcase and fished out something written by her brother.

The Portrait of a Historical Tide-Rider

Though he does not read much,
according to his ability in human peddling,
one can easily tell,
he once, perhaps, was the Party Secretary of a brigade,
or a chosen model in studying Mao's Thought,
well flattered by his commune members.

But today
the time has changed.
He is put in jail for an unpardonable crime:
Before selling other kids and females,
he sold his only son at a high price,
he sold his wife at a cheap price,
he sold his aged mother at a sale price.

The howling of his flesh could not buy a returning
                          glance from the father.
The tears of his spouse could not melt the heart of a True Man.
The mother, sold into a servant in an alien house, was silent.
Only she, she alone

could appreciate the unique heart of her filial son—
before plunging into the "sea,"
the strong found home for the weak.

A naive jailer
poked his conscience with curiosity.
True Man guffawed, with his open hairy chest:
"In this Era, if you do not seize money,
money seizes your life."

Before marching to the execution ground,
he asked for two roasted chickens.
Satiated with meat and wine,
he slept in contentedness like a baby.
In the whole world,
he alone realized his life-long wish:
Either before or after death
he has kept a clear conscience.

Although he does not read much,
he has grasped the spirit of two eras in the 20th Century.
He has been a never-falling-behind-tide-rider.

"It does not sound like a poem, but I like its satirical humor."

I felt very guilty, as if that poem caricatured me. I knew if I had stayed in China these years, I would not have been a bad tide-rider. Being Chinese means having a strong sense of historical trend. We follow whatever smells new. But the Chinese are Chinese; something in us will never change. For instance, the thrilling pleasure of watching beheadings and hearing firecrackers.

" Well, you look so smart in tight jeans. What are you doing now?"

"Today is Sunday; I just feel like a change. During the weekdays, I wear formal suits or whatever is suitable for a woman in public relations for a firm run by a Taiwanese. Let's go to a café and chat."

Li Jie became very cynical. She said she had been fired by three employers, if she did not adapt herself to fashions and cosmetics she would be fired again perhaps in a month. However, she was planning to start her own business. Then she told me a lot of stories about women of public relations. I cut her short and said I already knew from newspapers in Los Angeles and even drew a four-line sketch about them.

"Show it to me." Li Jie was still like an elder sister. If I refused, she was ready to poke my armpit and make me giggle.

"Here, read it by yourself."

A Lady of Public Relations

A woman succeeds in trade
By her beauty masquerades.
To realize modernizations by a curve
She surpasses Sai Jinghua in artifice.

"What does Sai Jinghua mean?"

"Literally it means 'surpassing the golden flower.' It is the name of a courtesan who expressed her patriotism through her adulterous affairs with Europeans. She saved Beijing from being completely ruined by these troops from eight countries at the end of the 19 Century. Don't tell me Chinese women do not know this?"

" Well, nobody is interested in books anymore. I guess one has to go abroad to study Chinese history. "

"Exactly. I learned much more about China and Chinese history in America than in China. Now I am an Assistant Professor of Chinese." Li was not impressed by my academic title. Casting an eye on my T-shirt, she said even a Chinese dog nowadays dresses better than an American. I laughed; American civilization is going inward while the Chinese are bursting outward. After having windowshopped around Huaihai Road and Nanjing Road, I was amazed that a dress could cost over 5,000 *yuan* and a dog of a special breed, 80,000 *yuan*.

I remembered a horrible tale Long had once told me. A woman with a master's degree from the Chinese department could not find a decent job and was cleaning hotels for little money. One day an illiterate country girl came and invited her to do business in the country, so that graduate student went with her. Can you guess what happened? That country girl sold her to a peasant as a wife.

"Is it a story or true, Jie?"

" True—everybody in China knows it. It was reported in an

official document. That woman was shut in a dark room for a couple of days and raped by that peasant."

"Absurd, absolutely absurd!"

"Have you heard from Lan lately?"

"No, she never wrote to me."

"She stopped writing to us four sisters in Shanghai after she married an 80-year-old man in New Zealand. Someone said the face of her husband is patched with old age spots, like a leper. "

Li uncapped her fountain pen and wrote:

A Woman's Pursuit

A woman only has pursuit
 but no longer possesses any value.
Why do you want to be married overseas,
 sleeping with that unfamiliar old and ugly?
In his luxurious house, how much space can you occupy?
If you cannot swim, what is the use of
waiting by that blue pool?

I laughed at her self-righteousness and wrote a retort on the side of Lan:

A Defense

In the old times, she was called
  "A Thousand-Pieces-of-Gold"
 but had no right to pursue.
Today she discards the "surface" value
  but gains liberty in "essence."
Why cannot I be married overseas,
 sleeping with that strange old and ugly?

A fly, with rights endowed by Heaven, can visit
 any luxurious house at will.
Why cannot I choose to
  sit by that blue pool,
   shedding Chang E's tears
    to my heart's content?

Li Jie slapped my back with a friendly palm. "You have been poisoned by the West."

"You haven't? Ha, ha—a deserter, running fifty steps away from the battleground, mocking the one who had run away a hundred steps."

"Our sister Mingxia is in the midst of her sixth divorce in the past five years. A shrewd career woman, but she has a nickname, 'Female Chen Shimei.'[5] She is not ashamed of her nickname at all. She even wrote a doggerel to pump up her courage."

Who Abandons Whom?

You, cursed males,
in the past thousands of years,
you, wagging your tongue and brushes,
pasted "beauty" on a woman's face,
raped her body and soul
            with "chastity."
Since "ugliness" and "evil"
            are the true nature of a human,
why cannot a woman have a share?
Ah, beat the drums of the New Era!
Light the torch of the Olympics!
Wait and see—
Who abandons whom, today?!

"What would you say about her doggerel?"

"Pretty good. But the idea has been plagiarized from the woman writer Zhang Kangkang. I saw her little article of the same title carried twice in the *Shenzhou Times* in Los Angeles."

"Without women like Mingxia in the first place, how could Zhang Kangkang have written that piece?"

After I left Shanghai I went straight to Qufu, the birthplace of Confucius. Several friends in America had asked me to pay tribute to the great sage of the world. When I arrived there, Qufu was crowded as though a country fair were in progress. A poem, scratched on the wall by a person attempting to immortalize his namelessness, informed me that Qufu was holding a beauty contest.

---

[5] In traditional Chinese drama, Chen Shimei is a typical ungrateful man who abandons his wife after his success at the imperial examination.

Beauty Contest in Qufu

Hundreds of beauties compete for Miss Qufu.
Confucian bridegrooms groan without body ailments.
Seeking codeless self no longer needs the Daoist Mount,
Every woman you meet in town is a Yu Xuanji.

Who is Yu Xuanji? Is she really alive today? Afraid of losing face, I went to the town library to check the name and easily found it in a dictionary of Chinese women poets.

Yu Xuanji is a Daoist poet of the Tang Dynasty. Seeking sexual liberty, she discarded her role of a man's concubine and resided in a Daoist nunnery on a mountain. She had many lovers and enjoyed traveling. Unfortunately, she was executed for beating her maid to death. She might have been wrongly prosecuted by a jealous male.

I hurried back to the hustle to find out who would win the Miss Qufu title. Alas, a few minutes too late. The contest was already over. It was hard to stop anyone in the dispersing crowd. When I went to the ladies' room, I saw a beautiful girl weeping in front of the bathroom mirror. She was definitely too narcissistic. An elderly lady told me that the girl had lost by two points. I felt enormous sympathy for her. I understood why she was crying. I cried when I got my English examination paper back and found a score of 98, rather than my goal of 100.

The elderly lady said she was heading for a Buddhist temple on a southern mountain tomorrow and invited me to go with her. I happily agreed, although I am agnostic. *La curiosité tue la femme.*

The trip was worthwhile. I learned that most of the young nuns escaped to nunneries because of setbacks in love or life. Surprisingly, a considerable number of them were college graduates. The more clearly you can see, the more pain you will bear. Life is indeed a sea of bitterness. The two most beautiful nuns I had talked with left their images permanently on my brain.

Beating the Wooden Fish

Although "sex" is no longer a forbidden zone,
she still presses her hand on that fig leaf.
Be cheated,
        be abandoned,
                be thrown into despair.
The culprit is not Him
    but that pure, noble love.

If she can be numb in the face of good and evil,
If she can cut the link between sex and love,
She can also take her natural beauty as "bid"
to plunge into the game, "Who abandons whom?"
Day day new,
    Endless pleasure.

Yet, being helplessly out of step with her age,
    she does not match her curved long hair.
Being hopelessly feudalistic,
        her suicide would pollute
              the rolling Yangtse River.
Being helplessly weak,
    she can only have her head shaved into a bulb and
beat the Wooden Fish in the Land of Death.

Counting the Buddhist Beads

Father cared too much.
Factory manager raped a female worker—
    Bilateral complicity.
Who needed your finger in their pie?

Mother was too sentimental.
Father was crushed by a revenging car;
who invited you to lose your temper
    and die of a heart attack?

Daughter was too filial.
Both parents had already passed away.
Love is gone at the loss of the body.
Why did you prosecute their killers?

Since you chose revenge,
why did you stop halfway,
Fleeing to a nunnery to seek a deceptive peace?
Can those thousand-year-old Buddhist Beads really
*   take off your ten thousand folds of hatred?*

"Long, are you back?" The noise from the front door inter-
rupts me.

"Did you bring today's newspaper?"

"Mei, take this paper to your mom."

"Mei, would you like to read me some from the paper?"

"What shall I read?"

"Anything you like."

Mei selects some short news that would interest a child—
contests on flowers and on pets.

"Mom, I need some time for my history project. It is due tomorrow."

"Okay, go and do your own things."

=
3
=

I continue my travel through the dream.

Being a scholar, I would like to attend Chinese conferences. I learned from a radio announcement that a literary conference was being held on the Miluo River, where Qu Yuan downed himself over two thousand years ago. When I rushed there, I found the conference participants eating Zongzi and dancing disco on the dragon pleasure boats. The conference was held to praise *Shanghun*—the "soul of commerce." How about *Guohun*—"the soul of the nation"? I asked the beaming scholars on the boats. They laughed, "*Guohun*? It left with Lu Xun, the father of modernism. Now we have entered the New Era, a postmodern era of money and pleasure." Their rude laughter made me feel out of place and out of time. Most Chinese writers are, like me, tide-riders. They always sing what the era requires them to. The very few subversive ones, like Qu Yuan, have to drown themselves with the stone of conscience around their necks. Their tragic deaths have brought about the merry-making of the majority.

I flew to Luoyang to attend a conference of the national floral society. This was a real conference. The speakers looked belligerent, with their sleeves folded well above their elbows. The purpose of this conference was to choose a national flower. The representatives from Luoyang insisted on the peony, those from Zhengzhou, the rose, those from Taiwan, the plum blossom. . . . One individual was for the orchid, another for the chrysanthemum. . . . The spokesman for the lotus won the upper hand by plagiarizing from classical prose, "I Love the Lotus." He said, "The peony stands for rebellion as well as wealth and money. In the Tang Dynasty, the peony was exiled to Luoyang because it disobeyed Emperor Wu Zetian's command to bloom in winter. Today the country needs stability and we cannot afford to elevate the peony. As for the chrysanthemum, it is a flower of the hermit, whose withdrawn spirit runs against the spirit of our Four Modernizations. The rose has not only been overused by Western poets but itself is too cheap, blooming every month and every day. Now I come to the point. We must chose the lotus as our national flower: empty stalk like a tube, upward, it stands erect; growing out of filthy silt, it touches no dust . . . ."

"I am strongly against the lotus. It stands for eroticism. Even foreigners know the female character called Golden Lotus. It captures the image of bound feet among Chinese women in old China."

"The orchid reminds people of Qu Yuan, a patriotic poet; but we know patriotism in fact is the product of provincialism. We Chinese must become the citizens of the world . . . ."

"Why do we need a national flower then?" Whistles and curses arose from the audience.

After a three-day, three-night roundtable discussion, the conference finally selected the plum blossom as China's national flower. The representatives from Taiwan jumped for joy. Well, not too soon. Their joy reminded the conference Chair of something. He cleared his throat and said to the whole audience, "I am sorry that we cannot choose the plum blossom as the national flower of China, because it will stir up a political issue. The plum blossom has been the national flower of Taiwan all along. Choosing it would mean Taiwan's domination over the mainland; choosing another flower would mean our support for a Two-China policy. I would advise flower-lovers to stay away from politics." I had experienced the excitement, anger, agitation of a listener. But alas, much ado about nothing, as meaningless as any conference can be.

I rushed to a national pet convention in Guangzhou. This time I was determined not to be a mere listener, even though I was a bit late. It was already the last day of a five-day convention. But, of course, the final events were more interesting. One male speaker, in a long skirt, talked vehemently about why he believed the rooster should be China's national pet. He demonstrated how the map of China is shaped like a rooster, how Chinese civilization woke up world civilization like a rooster, and this year is the year of the rooster—even America has issued stamps of Chinese roosters. Rooster—hope. Does our nation need hope? Many listeners nodded their heads.

But the spokesman for the dragon would not give up, even though some young intellectuals had proved it a symbol for tyranny. He said that it was wrong for the gullible public to use the panda as a Chinese pet, giving it to different countries for display. The panda used to be a tough animal, eating iron according to its historical record; but it has pitifully degenerated into a squishy mixture of teddy bear and cute kitten, a weak vegetarian. What's the use of roosters in our postmodern era? Roosters are going to disappear by the twenty-first century. Only hens have a right to sit and lay eggs in battery boxes on chicken farms. . . .

Suddenly I saw two cockroaches in the super clean hotel. I was amazed at how they could survive there. I stood up and recited my speech in an emotional voice:

AN ODE TO ROACHES
Infinity of Emptiness

Roaches, the mystery of life,
old as dinosaurs,
going to survive for another million or billion years.
You are far too intelligent
to confront me—
a million times bigger monster.
What's the use of struggling?
When I smear you I cannot feel any wetness on my thumb.
When I crush you I cannot see anything red.
You should make me feel the cruelty of a slaughter;
yet no horror of bloodshed,
no sign of pain,
no sound of complaint,
no wriggling of the body,
no twist of the skin.
During daylight you maneuver in dark corners.
At night you swarm around the sink,
absolutely mute.
No one should have noticed your existence;
yet I found out in the encyclopedia
you can chew anything— garbage, soap, book bindings,
even telephone wires!
Not even bombs can wipe out your cockroach babies—
immune to human poison.
Roaches, oh roaches,
old as the dinosaurs,
going to live another million or billion years,
outlaugh all human life of meaningfulness.

Perhaps because my speech was a sort of poem, which tells the truth indirectly, the whole audience was persuaded except for one man who had a sober head on his shoulders.

"What is your subtitle?"

I regretted this at once. Why should I have told them the sub-title at all? In my dilemma, Zhuang Zi appeared with two cock-roaches in his hand: one was dusty as if coming from a filthy latrine pit; another black and shiny, undoubtedly coming from the West or a Westernized place. The two roaches chorused: "If you are not a roach, how can you know my life is meaningless?" The whole audience got the insight and voted unanimously for the roach as China's national pet.

Xiao Fan patted my shoulder like an old pal.

"Yun, a great job. I love the insinuations of your Ode. Ha, ha, Chinese civilization is older than dinosaurs. We have mutely survived and we are going to live another million or bil-lion years, meaningful or meaningless. . . ."

"That is your misreading. I did not know those implica-tions. My inspiration was just aroused by the two cockroaches I saw in the hotel."

After Fan left, I climbed to each balcony of the hotel to experi-ence the different visions of the horizon.

> *In front*
> *there seems*
>   *a dead line*
> *I know it can't be dead*
>   *only the breath-span of my vision*

> *I want to draw a*
> *dead-line for my*
>   *melancholy*
> *to prove my power*
>   *over*
>   *eternity*

> *The higher I rise in*
>   *the aloof tower*
> *the line retreats*
>   *further apart*
>   *I want to pin it dead there*
> *the only way is to stop here*

The skyline
I strive to reach
is merely
an optical
disease

The horizon
not straight
a hoop of seasons
renews
nothing
new.

My unexpected success stops my daydreaming.

"Dinner is ready!" Long calls from the kitchen.

"Mei, go have dinner with your father. Today is our Chinese New Year's Eve. Sorry, I am too weak to join you. Enjoy your meal."

=
4
=

Oh, it is already dark. The rain is pouring again. The pattering on the roof is trying hard to imitate Chinese firecrackers.

I feel very guilty, as if I have brought the rain to the west coast. Before I came to Los Angeles for my campus interview, I asked the Chairman, "What should I bring with me?"

"An umbrella."

My old colleagues laughed, "Don't you know California has had a five-year drought by now? The state is collapsing. We hope you have enough water to drink." When I stepped out of the airplane with my family on August 15 in the year of 1991, Los Angeles was gray with a misty drizzling. "A lot of accidents today on the freeway. With a long drought, people here forget how to drive in the rain," the taxi driver told me excitedly. When I went to buy a house, my agent told me, "Never mind the roof—in California we have sunny days all the time." Last winter it did rain and I had to spend seven hundred dollars to repair the roof. This winter, the rain becomes wild as if it has collected all my tears for Ramon and is having a hearty release.

But I have not wept in the past seven months. My eyes are burning hot with overwork, my hips sore with oversitting, and my back aching with overdreaming in bed.

To live, one must keep thinking the opposite.

The first summer we spent in Los Angeles was truly hot. For the first five days, I felt utterly imprisoned. No cash. The bank said they would not give us cash for a cashier's check from another state. Well, we had to live meagerly on fifty dollars.

Why did I choose the smog of Los Angeles, not the paradise of Hawaii? Human perversity, I guess. I was lying on the floor of apartment C along Garvey Avenue for the seventh night. The traffic was zooming day and night. I dared not open the window. When I popped my head out to see the gray sky in the evening, I would see a middle-aged tree in the palm-sized concrete backyard. It still had green leaves below its shoulders but above its neck was nothing but frizzy dry white hair. I was sure it was the masterpiece of smog. Who asked that tree to pop its head above the protected wall? If she were a professor in China, her gray hair would earn more respect from ignorant people. But in America, gray is the color of shame one is only too anxious to hide. I looked at myself in the mirror, and the gray hairs were too numerous to pluck out. Who said that if one hair is plucked a hundred will grow?

There was no furniture in the apartment. My husband, daughter, and I all slept on the floor. It was not bad. I recalled my days in the countryside of China. About thirty girls squeezed in a straw-thatched room during the winter. We all slept on the earthen floor covered with rice straw. It was cozy since we were packed tight like sardines. We felt excited to leave home. When I woke up at night, I could hear Li crying for her parents, Zhang mumbling in a nightmare, Yang giggling, Su singing Peking opera, Ma snoring, Wu grinding her teeth. . . . I was not scared. No matter what you heard they were human noises.

One car zoomed by, two, three, four, five. . . . A screaming police car interrupted my count. Why should I have counted them in the first place? When you cannot sleep, it is better to count jumping sheep.

For the sixth time I ran to the bathroom. I did not eat much tonight. How many times do I have to get up again? Ten minutes later I went to the bathroom again. In earlier times, I had done it in the dark, afraid of awakening my husband and child in the other room. This time, I shut the door and turned on the light to have a close examination of what was coming out of my stomach. Dear me, everything was still in its undigested original shape: red tomato, green cucumber, white rice. . . . My digestive system had completely lost its function. The waste dropped into the water of the toilet bowel, instantly loosening apart. Not even a bad smell. An ancient Chinese joke says if a human fart does not smell, it foretells a person's death.

I was scared. What kind of disease do I have now?

I had been sick for six weeks and I felt no hope of getting better. It had started with an itchy throat and low fever, then a light cough, a worsening cough. A cold, or a flu, something come and gone, never worth much attention. Yet it refused to go this time. Perhaps I had overworked myself during the moving. Long was really a good-for-nothing. Although he was fired three months ago when his boss learned I got a job in California, he could not help me much. Every box he packed had to be repacked.

Although he had more physical strength than I he did not exert himself that much. He could not even wring a wash towel dry. It was always dripping, dripping.

I did not bother to draw the night curtain. When the window turned gray I got up and tried to type a letter to my sister in Beijing. Feeling weak, I laid down again. Moreover, I was too spoiled by America to work on the small computer on the floor. Kneeling on the carpet or sitting on a pillow was becoming too much for me.

At last, I could draw my money from Omni Bank. About ten o'clock, I went out to search for a suitable used car. I could not drive very well, nor could my husband. But we must buy a car. We must drive. Driving is a matter of survival in Los Angeles.

Doctor Yang came. He used to be a famous doctor of traditional Chinese medicine but now was a car dealer.

"What is a salvaged car?"

"A car destroyed at least 70% beyond normal repair. I did that sort of business when I first came here, penniless. It is a deceptive business that my conscience forbids me to do anymore."

"Then we are fortunate to have met you. Pity, I lost a $150 deposit to that evil Mr. Lu. I learned he was also from mainland China. How could he do that to his own countrymen?

" Would you please show me the original paper for this car before I sign?

"Why is it that you said you bought it originally for $6,000, but the paper shows you paid only $4,900?"

" Well, let me see. Ah, I blotched out this but forgot that one. Okay, you are right. You may pay me only $7,000 for the car. You know this includes tax, registration, all sorts of costs."

" Would you like to have lunch with us? Simple noodles."

"Okay. I am tired of restaurant food."

"Doctor Yang, do you know the symptoms of AIDS?"

" Yes. Why? Is a friend suffering from this incurable disease?"

"No, I was reading a newspaper before you came. It seems a fatal disease."

"Not seems. It is."

Every symptom Doctor Yang described to me fit my own condition. After he left I shut my bedroom door, thinking hard.

How could I possibly get this disease? From Prues? He once said a gay professor had been interested in him. Prues was a yielding man. No. It must be that disgusting man I met at a party in Dallas. When I undressed, his male organ shrank.

Still, he crawled upon me and lingered for one minute. I was sure it was him. So disgusting. He even had the audacity to say, "Big, isn't it." No, it could not be him, because I did not have real contact with him. Was it Chris, the last man I had bodily contact with? A sweet person, who kept saying, "How could I have missed you the past three years?" No, it was not him. How could AIDS burst out so quickly? Moreover, I had started to cough before I met him. If I had AIDS, I must have sinned against him by passing HIV to his body. A poor good man, with five kids.

What should I do before I die? My daughter was only eleven years old and my Long could not speak English. Luckily, I had not had sex with Long in the past twelve months. I had never expected the price of separating sex from love and morals to be that high.

I walked downstairs.

"Where are you going?" Long was cooking again. Three meals a day, a good occupation for a man.

"I want to try our car. "

I drove the car around the parking lot twice and raced out of the gate. When I got to the freeway, two cars hooted. It was dangerous indeed. But I got on the freeway; I was free! I knew I could drive if I had the nerve. Two months ago I drove my family in a rental car to see Niagara Falls, because we were moving away from the east coast. On the way I first drove the wrong way into a one-way street and then had a small collision. The accident only cost American Express $470, but my nerves had been broken. Now I had finally gotten over the fear.

"Long, are you ready to learn to drive tomorrow?"

He was more timid than ever. On the way back from Buffalo, I had merely let him try for a half hour on a local road, but he was caught by the police as a "drunkard" and got a ticket for 80 dollars.

"I would like to wait a couple of days. I am not feeling very well."

"All right. You may sit in the back and watch me drive first."

Daytime was easier for a dying lady. I could still drag my body around to do something. But night was long and suffocating. I felt so depressed that my brain was congealing into lead.

A walking Tomb
Smog of numb darkness

Breathes out
Darting tongues of a coiled cobra
From the hemisphere tightly
Pressed on the
Ground

A bright ribbon buckles tawny hair
White daisies rim the moss of grief-stone
   Inside lies
Bean curd of brain
Condensed in a coupled vacuum
Could two strong horses pull its two halves apart?

A round lead of infinite death
Is sinking
Not in the sea of water
But in the solid mass of cold dust,
   hot rocks, slimy petroleum, and
    gas of indigestion
Dazedly drowsing in drowning. . . .

The following day I felt very weak. My body seemed to stagnate before I had the chance to die.

   I do not know whether I am alive
    such gravity of inertia
    no more wish to move
    absolutely still
    a boat in the dead sea

  A deadened feeling of self-abandoning
    no edge of hunger
    no sense of boredom
   A strange touch of death
    kisses me
   binds me like a web of spider

   I wish I could hate somebody
   I wish I could love somebody
  Why don't I have the courage of a criminal?
  Was I born to be anchored in the sluggish pool?

Wind, for whom do you
blow blow blow?!
Please slash open my blood vessels
so my life will scream and flow
again

My
life is numb
like a bag of sawdust
The boxer says he prefers to punch a sandbag
not me
Perhaps I need to pay someone to
make my sloth body dangle
one two
one two
one two three

I read my scribble a couple of times and giggled. It was nice that I still had a comic sense before I went to my grave.

A month to go before my job started at the University of Southern California. So much time to ruminate. As my mood was gloomy, all the sad memories welled up. Although I had been looked upon by some as a free spirit, I was eventually left a lonely woman. I recalled a moment of crisis in my life. That day happened to be June 4th. A lot of blood shed on Tian An Men Square. I was called up by the FBI for information I might have from my letters from China. I told them my father had died and I had not had letters from home in the past three months. It was true. The Chinese Students Association asked me to join their demonstration in front of the Chinese Embassy in Washington. I declined and merely wrote them a $50 check. I was too timid to be involved in real politics. I said goodbye to Prues and Long had signed our divorce papers.

I had been coughing for three weeks. Helen called me and said she was diagnosed as a T.B. patient and her doctor had advised her to send all her friends for a skin test. I went to the clinic. The result was positive. Well, I thought the T.B. test was largely intended for Chinese immigrants. But ironically, Helen, my friend from England, turned mine from negative to positive. That did not bother me much. Once it is positive it is positive for life, the doctor says. No more tests for the rest of my life. Anyway, T. B. is curable.

The Chinese graduate student in the department jumped at

me and accused me of following her everywhere. *Where are you?* I was confused because lately I was so preoccupied with my own trouble that I had not even noticed her. Her undertone accused me of lesbianism. Dear God, how knowledge had abandoned human beings to dogs. When I was in China I had the freedom to hold a woman's hand and Chinese women love to hold each other's hands or put their hands on each other's shoulders. But I was told in Britain that a woman cannot hold a woman's hand in public and holding the hand of the opposite sex is perfectly normal. Now I could not even look at a woman. I remember I instantly turned myself away from an intelligent woman when she said her mother warned her that she would be involved with a lesbian this month. I could not figure out whether this was a seduction or a warning. Nevertheless, the supersensitivity in America had obviously ghettoized every individual being.

The Chair had another personal talk with me because the Chinese graduate student had reported that I was doing the same research topic she was doing. *What is her topic? On hell. Go to hell, then.* She was paranoid, perhaps overpressed by her doctoral exams. One minute she jumped at me for two books missing from her office; another minute she apologized, saying she'd found her books in her apartment. Her paranoia drove me crazy.

I went home and saw two roaches in the kitchen. The apartment I was living in looked still new but was already infested with roaches. Life suddenly revealed its utter meaninglessness to me. I studied hard in China because I believed I was studying for revolution; I worked hard in the fields because I believed I was producing food for the people; I taught hard in China, because I had a country. Now there was nothing. The utopian belief in revolution was gone with the wind. Gullible people who had slaved for revolution now were prone at the foot of the fetish of money. Rumors circulated—anyone returning to China would be examined for counter-revolutionary activities, even thoughts, and there were spies on campus. It had been three months since I had had a letter from China. Where is home? Where is my motherland? Where is my father? My father died four months ago. Father, could you forgive me now for not going home to see my grandma when she was dying of cancer? I could have gone home if I had not been led by the zest of making revolution on the farm.

Apart from the mechanical writing of papers for classes, I

spent most of my time staring at roaches. They were crawling on the bedroom walls now. When I walked in the living room I could feel the army of roaches following me like mice. If I cooked in the kitchen, the roaches lay in wait for any crumbs or droppings. About two months ago, I phoned the landlady to have the exterminators come. They came and the poison did not work. I launched war against roaches at midnight by suddenly turning on the light. There were simply too many. I recognized my defeat. I even started to compromise with the roaches, admiring their spirit. Finally I lifted my fingers and wrote a poem to honor them (the ode I recited at the national pet convention).

After scribbling this ode on the toilet tissue, I went to bed for more sleep, gloves on and cotton balls in my ears to avoid the roaches' revenge against me. In the twilight zone of my brain, Zhuang Zi whispered to me: "If you are not a roach, how can you know a roach's life is not meaningful?"

> *Terror*
> *Is*
> *Not a thunder-bolted crown*
> *Not a lightning-cleft heart*
> *But caterpillars of*
> *An uncurable numbness*
> *Crawling on the tired body of*
> *Life.*

Right! Living itself is meaning. If I am to die, my husband and child must live a better and healthier life.

I got up from the floor and went out to buy a *World Daily* in Chinese. I made many phone calls trying to find a job for Long. Fortunately, we had come to Los Angeles where the Chinese can survive without knowing English.

I saw an ad for a house which said that owning was cheaper than renting an apartment. Great, my daughter and husband must move out of that coffin-like apartment.

I phoned the agent, a friendly Shanghainese named Wang. He persuaded me to buy a five-bedroom house. His reasoning was watertight, logical, and I was always gullible. So I took the house immediately. In the following days I was busy signing papers for a mortgage, buying furniture, getting my daughter settled in a nearby elementary school. What a good busy-ness—

I completely forgot that I was dying. I did not notice when my cough, which had lasted for two months, had gone.

As soon as I moved into the house, I met with an insurance agent to buy a $200,000 life policy. If I had the nerve to run into a car the day I died, my dependents would get $400,000. Fortunately, I did not know the insurance company had to check blood for HIV; otherwise, I would not have dared to buy life insurance at all. When the health report came, I was completely relieved. I did not have the AIDS virus and I felt perfectly recovered from my sickness. Ready to start a new job!

=

5

=

"Mom, are you dreaming again?"

"No, I was just thinking of the past."

"My birthday is coming. You promised to have my poems edited and published by the Mom Press. Are you still going to do it for me?"

"Yes, of course. Bring all your poems here. I will ask a real poet to write you a foreword."

My daughter has been replacing me now. During my last conference in New York, she insisted on sleeping in the queen-sized bed in my crowded "bathroom." She has been writing poems almost daily since the day I stopped writing. In the evenings we often take a walk. She always hangs close to me like a lover.

—Please keep some distance from me. I need to breathe.

—Why can't you take me as your boyfriend?

—My boyfriend?

—No, Mom. I want you to be my boyfriend.

I understand she is growing into a lady now.

—Do any boys like you in your class?

—Yes. But I do not like them that much. Mom, you taught me that men are weak, lack emotion, stupid, ...

— I never said that.

—But that is what you think of my father.

Have I? Did I? Do I? I want to tell Mei that her father is a great man, a loving man, an industrious man, the best man in the world. But I know Mei will not believe me. It is hard to believe the truth if you have been brought up with lies.

How did I get to know Long?

It was like a pastoral utopia, waves of wheat were beating the banks of fields, bees and butterflies playing hide-and-seek in the blooming yellow rapeseeds. A group of six college graduate students were harvesting wheat.

"Hey! Yun, look at Long. He has been gazing at you from time to time."

"Hey— Long! Work harder. Don't cut off your fingers."

Of the six graduate students, only Long and I were

unmarried.

The moon was like a sickle. I went to a pond to wash my sweat-soaked clothes. He was there, too.

"Shall I help you with the basin?"

He was a shy man. It was almost the first time I had heard his voice. It was hard to refuse.

He hung my clothes one by one on the line in the yard.

The following day was a Sunday. All the married graduates went home.

We were alone in the dorm. He disappeared in the morning. When he came back in the evening he brought me peaches, apricots, and a bunch of white tulips. He said his home was in a village about ten miles away. I was moved by his tender care, as no men had showed me much tenderness before. I felt the love trauma left by Jiang hurting me again. That night I wrote a letter to Feng and agreed to marry him. But a week later, his letter informed me that because it had been too painful to live when I rejected him a month ago, he had saved himself from insanity by marrying the girl he had rejected earlier. What a life!

When another holiday came, Long invited me to his village. According to the custom, an agreement to go would admit a relationship or an informal engagement. I did go with him. His family looked extremely poor compared with other villagers. Other houses had tiles or cogon grass but his was covered with rice straw. His father had to patch the roof after each rain. Everybody knew that I was the daughter of a senior cadre, at least at the rank of the county mayor. My status made some young men hesitate to ask for my hand. That Long had the nerve to love me made him different from others.

At that time I suffered setbacks in my career as well as in love. I was selected to teach at my university after graduation. But an official document about Chaonong sent everyone back home.[6] Before I went to college, I was a farmer in the Dabie Mountains and so I was sent back there. Then, I was a woman with high aspirations. I hated to waste my youth not doing something for the people and the country. Being unable to teach the English I had learned, I volunteered to give up my salary and stay in the countryside to teach the peasants. Long supported whatever I chose to do. He said to me: "Now you are strong enough to support yourself by work points. When you get old, I

---

[6] Chaonong refers to Chaoyang Agricultural College that advocated the policy of sending students after graduation back to where they had come from.

will support you." He was assigned to teach in a junior-high school of the county. I was moved by his simplicity and honesty. I thought of Jiang and suspected that the reason he had given for abandoning me was not true. The truth was that I had to go back to countryside and he was a garrison guard in the city.

I wrote a couple of poems for Long and he wrote a couple back. His seemed fresh and new. I started to be fond of him. Even though he did not look very intelligent, he was no doubt an uncarved wood, reserving its original wholeness. In those hard times in the countryside, I labored in the fields during the day and taught peasants to read and write at night. I often ate nothing but plain rice. Long would come to see me every weekend, bringing me a sack of turnips or cabbage. He would sit by my side, warming my frostbitten hands. The first night he kissed me I cried. I was torn between a desire to marry him and a strong will to make revolution.

One night I dreamt that an old granny came to see me. She asked me whether I still wanted to study. I said eagerly, "Yes, particularly English. I have a BA in English and I love English. But I just don't know how to use my English to serve the people." She disappeared without leaving me an answer.

Three days later I was informed by the authority that I should have a physical examination in town. Then I was told that the Educational Bureau in Beijing had decided to send me to study English in Britain. The day I left the Dabie Mountains, Long looked every sad. In his dream he saw me change into a rabbit and run away from him. His colleagues persuaded him to give up on me and marry a local girl. He would not listen but volunteered to go teach Chinese in Tibet for two years. When Jiang heard the news that I was going abroad he wrote a letter to me, implying that we could resume our old friendship. But I wrote him back, and told him that I would not abandon Long, who had loved me and supported me when I was a peasant.

Nevertheless, I was tortured by my attachment to Long since I did not really have any passion for him. We did not seem to have a common language. Apart from my respect for his virtues I found nothing between us. I struggled and struggled and finally decided to break up with him after I returned from Britain. But when I saw how much he suffered—his head swung helplessly like a madman—my heart melted. Considering all his virtues, I signed the marriage certificate.

As expected, my marriage has been miserable from its first day. We could not talk. He never wrote me another poem.

Perhaps the two poems seemed original and fresh because he had not read any poetry in his life. We could make love, we could have a child, but I refused to kiss him. I simply could not. Mei has witnessed my suffering. I do not tell lies. But since I chose the bitter fruit, I should try to make it more tolerable for swallowing.

My brain starts to blur into the future.

"Ladies and Gentleman:
Today we have Yun Hu, a distinguished woman from the Earth, to give us a talk on her philosophy of marriage. Let's give her a warm welcome."

Thunderous applause.

" Well, every word I am going to tell you today is not from books but from my personal experience." Applause.

"If you want a dependable, secure marriage, you should never marry a man or a woman you love. Marriage has nothing to do with love. Marriage should be a form of cooperation for survival. That is what my husband Long and I have found out. Like the Mosuo Community on the border of the Sichuan province in China, marriage, or simply a family, does not have any authority about personal life such as sexual love, political stand, or professional career. You may think it is largely economic cooperation. Well, it is. But it does not mean the money made by the husband and wife has to be put together. Each has a bank account so each feels economic independence. I pay for the house and my husband pays for food. This week I give Mei thirty dollars; next week he gives her ten. We have no quarrels over money. I have a lot of extramarital lovers, while my husband has none. When I asked him to take some and told him life would be pretty dull having contact with only one person and one body, he replied with a smile: 'It is my personal choice.' So our equality lies in our equal freedom of choice. It took a long time for us to be open-minded and tolerant of each other, but we finally succeeded. Now I still do not love my husband. Love is enclosure. Because I do not love him, my wild passion enables me to reach different beings in this world. Sometimes, I feel sorry for my husband. He loves me and his love blocks him from all other women. If our marriage is a mistake, it is his mistake, not mine. Last week at the banquet for our thirtieth wedding anniversary, I told him: 'Feel free to have a divorce anytime you want.' I will not call my marriage happy, but it is tolerable. As I advance in my career, finance, status, I tend to have more lovers. I tend to forget him or hate him. But when I am sick or having bad luck, I know I am falling down on a mattress, not a hard rock." Big laugh from the audience.

About six months after my talk, that planet sent me a huge medal—a sort of Nobel prize from their planet. Their letter of thanks said that their rate of divorce had dropped thirty percent after my talk.

Happiness again sobers me.

"Mei, what are you doing? Are you going to show me your poems?"

"I am coming. I have been revising a poem that I am afraid you will not like."

"Please read that one to me."

> *Freedom is individuality.*
>   *If*
> *Individuality is selfishness,*
>   *Then*
> *Freedom is You.*
>   *Why*
> *Can't I Be Us? Because*
> *You steal, invade, and take over*
> *Till I disintegrate and disappear*
> *To make another replica of You.*
> *I am selfish, too.*
> *But we can never be two,*
> *Unless Me equals You.*

A feeling of relief swept over my heart. "Mei, I am happy for you. You have grown up and are yourself now."

You are right, Mei. I am guilty of being selfish. Before you were five, when you needed a mother to cling to most, I abandoned you to your grandma, your aunt, and your father for my own career. The day I left for Shanghai, you grabbed me, calling me a bad mother.

> *She's only three*
> *Her little fingers circled my throat*
> *   like a gold necklace*
> *   only locked too tight*
> *Tighter and tighter it went*

I was forced to beat her buttocks
        She refused to let me go
My nail pricked her tender skin
        like a thorn
She released her baby chain
With tears in her
            raven eyes she
said, "A bad mother, people say!"
Walked away like a demonstrator
                with her aunt
A scarlet badge
        seared on my professional heart.

"Mom, I love you. I feel very lucky to have you as a model. But I feel I need my independence now."

"Yes, it is time you set sail on your own wings."

"Goodnight, Mom."

"Goodnight."

=
6
=

After so much defecation, I feel my body being purified and my heart becoming tender and the world rosy. To love is beautiful; to live is meaningful.

My first memory of the world is of green fields and the golden sun. My father was shouldering my elder sister and me in two baskets with a long pole. My mother was riding on a donkey. Everybody was laughing. My sister and I flying up and down in turn, like being on a swing.

A big part of my life fits perfectly into the cliché: "being born in New China and growing up under the Red Flag." But unexpectedly, an ideal system, once established, had bred its own grave-diggers. I went to elementary school in 1957. One day my sister came back from her boarding school and whispered to me: In the West everybody is equal before the law and no parent has the right to beat a child. My thin body was trembling like a reed in the wind. Although I did not even know where the West was, I wrote my first big character poster.

> *My father gave me five cents to buy vinegar. I ran very fast. When I got to the store I found my pocket had a hole in it and the five cents was gone. My father beat me. Down with his tyranny!*

Two years later, one summer afternoon, my father mumbled two words to me like a mosquito.

"What?" I asked.

He mumbled again.

"What?"

"Where are your ears?" He slapped my face.

Being too short to get to his face, I slapped his pot belly. He kicked me and I yelled, "Better leave a scar on my leg so that I can renew my hatred for you like a farmhand to a landlord whenever I see it."

Having trampled landlords in China to the ground, my father was so enraged by my comparison that he beat me black and blue with a club. At dinnertime he told the family a joke.

> *One day the master wanted to set up his mosquito-*
> *net for the summer and asked his servant to buy some*
> *Zhugan (bamboo sticks). An hour later the servant*
> *came back with a basket and showed the master the*
> *Zhugan (pig liver) he had bought.*
> *"Where are your ears?" asked the master.*
> *"Here." The servant took out the pig ears he had hid-*
> *den in his large pocket.*
> *"How did you know I'd also bought the ears,*
> *Master?"*

The whole family laughed. But I refused to forgive him for
his glib tongue. From then on when he beat me I always beat
back. I was known in the county as "a girl who dares to beat the
mayor." Soon my father stopped beating children because all
my brothers and sisters learned to beat back.

One day in 1958, I pointed to the three huge characters on the
wall and asked my big brother what they meant. He ran a step
forward and turned a somersault, shouting: "Big—Leap—
Forward!" Soon my family cracked our cooking pots and we ate
in public dining halls. I finally got the chance to experience
how Oliver Twist wants more. I loved the campaigns of killing
flies and sparrows. I still remember the laughable scene in
which Uncle Du, with a magnifying glass, tried to find maggots
in dried manure. When he failed he offered me fifty cents to
buy twenty maggots from my small box. I refused, because I had
promised to hand in fifty maggots to my teacher the following
day. Oh, how I loved the sparrow meat cooked with bean curd by
my brother. But later he told me, because all the birds were
killed, the crops suffered from insects. The following year we
did not have enough grain to eat. We ate all sorts of tree leaves.
I remember the trees were still sprouting in the fall. And we forgot the taste of meat. But we felt stronger without meat; we were
told that all of the meat went to pay our debt to the Russians. The
Russians were much poorer than us. In one of our plays, it was
said that they only ate stars and the moon.

How could one only see the Cultural Revolution as horrible
as "flood and monsters." It was also a once-in-a-thousand-
years good time for the youth. We traveled free all over the country. My elder sister fought back at her high school and asked her
principal face to face why he had written a black letter to our

parents.   No more classes, no more exams.   We danced, we sang.   Every day was exciting like a festival.   We learned what the books could never have taught us.

Why did my mother shed tears the day I left for the country-side?   I knew I was born flimsy.   The first time I carried a shoulder pole, no more than fifty pounds, my face turned ghastly pale. When I was sent to the clinic, the nurse could not find my pulse. I gained the name of "Bourgeois Miss."   But three years' labor forged me into a strong horse.   During the last harvest before I left the farm, I beat everyone in carrying bundles of rice.   When I climbed the groaning ladder to the top of the high stacks, I stood, with a pointed shoulder pole in hand, looking down at the exhausted young men on the ground.   My heart started to throb: "The time has changed;   men and women become equal.   What a man can do a woman can also do."   What a man cannot do a woman can also do.

I enjoyed open-door schooling during my college days.   In Luoyang Tractor Factory, I saw for the first time a worker who stood on one spot screwing bolts on the assembly line all day long and all year round—how fearful to be a screw on the revolutionary machine.   Even now when I want to show off my English vocabulary, I will ask an American, "Do you know the word 'paulownia'?"   Ha, ha, you don't know.   I learned this English word during my open-door schooling in a village surrounded by paulownia trees.

You think that I oppose the current Chinese Reform because of my sentiments for the victimized women and children.   No, you are wrong.   After 1949, China had been distilled into a pond of purified water and its people penned to the age of innocence. Reform has at least opened the dams and washed the nation to the open sea. Stirring, risky, promising.   Life, like love, is an adventure in its natural form.   Great order comes out of great chaos.

China, to other people, may have been a hell, but for me it has been a utopia.   I love China, its past, present, and future.

Why don't you return to China?   Good question.   It won't be a riddle if you have read Henry James' *Portrait of A Lady* and understand why Isabel chose to marry Osmond.

One day I went to the Immigration and Naturalization Service to inquire how long it would take me to become an American citizen.   "Six years?   Why so long?"   The young officer looked at me and said with a funny smile, "For psychological adjustment." Perhaps he was joking with me but I took his words seriously. I had been suffering an inferiority complex in America because of my alien status. In China every citizen is taught to become the master of the country by strangling the master of the self; but in America there is no master of the country but the master of each individual. But I did not realize this then. My eagerness to get American citizenship was actually my attempt to cure my psychological problem caused by that lingering illusion of being the master of the country. I might feel intellectually superior to some poorly educated Americans, but I felt inferior to all Americans, regardless their skin-color, age, or sex. When I went out of the INS building, a black woman shouted at me because I had parked my car in the wrong place and blocked her way. I apologized to her like a concubine to the master. But she kept screaming. I finally shouted back: "Fuck you!" She was first stunned and then laughed, friendly. *See, Americans really teach women how to fuck.* Then we chatted for a while. When she learned that I had a daughter, she said she was teaching Modern Dance at the YWCA in Covina. "Take your daughter there and I'll teach her how to sway her hips."

Why do I feel the world is so beautiful tonight? Am I dying? I can feel my love fragmenting at the moment, just like the love of that funny Edward at Urbana. I seem to be waiting for somebody. Is it Ramon?
Perhaps.

perhaps the eagle is not in good shape
perhaps the seagull is away again
perhaps the penguin is shunning an imagined death
perhaps the swan is no longer able to visit the earth
perhaps the open-mouthed frog is waiting for
                    another line of raindrops
perhaps the sensitive plant feels nothing when over-touched
perhaps it is time for the dandelion
          to outgrow her downy naivete
                    shaving all her hair of anxieties off
                         to become a true bald soprano
perhaps that is the last signpost in the sea:
          care ceases when the light of waiting burns out.

Oh, I love Ramon, I love Simon, I love Edward, I love Marios, I love Bob, I love Sun, I love Tony, I love Prues and

Karen, I love Dryle and Marlowe, I love Mao and Deng, and I love Meng in spite of our rivalry. I must restate that when I made love with Meng it was not merely a political gesture.

Door and blinds shut
In utter claustrophobia
At the moment Heaven and Earth merge
On the spot where the sun and the moon meet
Eyes slanting down
Hands groping up
A sudden spray of twilight
From the sea of dark blue air
A huge baby whale
Hurled itself to suck the single Amazonian breast
My fingers caress its twitching tail
Its diaper wets
I've found no whale but a penguin
Under its swallowtail
The same whiteness
Touches our reciprocal thrill.

I love all harmless sexual attractions.

Accidentally I catch his eye or he catches mine
An inexpressible communion flows
as if falling in love at the first sight
I deliberately turn away
Then curiously I turn to see he is still gazing at me
My heart throbs
huddling itself behind my marital shield
Yet irresistibly my body melts
by the melodious voice of the merman
Nothing more than the voluptuous sea
that can so easily seduce me
I love his gentle, amiable face
though wrinkled, beaming with tenderness
He loves reading, having read too much
furrowed his brow carelessly with the increase of knowledge
I used to loathe baldness so much
Now I love him to the touch
Although I hate hairy bodies
seeing his naked arms and legs
covered with yellow grass of a long drought

I have a longing to touch them no matter how rough
His eyes betray a stronger desire to caress me.

I am entirely different from him. My skin, my hair, my voice, my tongue. Yet it must be the difference that has bewitched us. But difference is a lovable monster. We both painfully shun one another.

We were together, on and off, for three weeks. When I was alone, I chanted his name like a witch. I was certain he heard me. When we were parting, we knew we would never see each other again. He is mine as I am his—a fantasy that tickles life with needles of pleasurable pain.

Perhaps you will think that I love all men indiscriminately. Actually I am very choosy. When I love a man, I appreciate his words. My lover must be a poet, a player with words that excite my spiritual orgasm. Then I ignore all norms, morality. I play with him in primal language in the intertwining of our yin and yang birds. My love involves a lover's service or obligation. My lover is my proofreader in the making. Once he sees my body concealed in the civilized trappings, he is obliged to read my words. I am unable to produce a thrill without the artillery of a shared language (which can be utterly different. I love difference.)

Once you read my body, you must read my words. I loathe a man who is only interested in the transparency of the skin.

For most, the more illicit, the more pleasure the love can engender. For me, love is forever original and personal. I do not want voyeurs to steal our pleasure. I can only make love in the freedom of the dark sea. Without the sense of freedom at the right moment, I would be too rigid to spread my legs apart.

I am a charioteer, forever pulling apart in two opposite directions. When I am climbing up, my feet are stepping down. I am a tree, whose branches are stretching into the sky and roots are striking down into the earth.

Who says I am *yin*, a passive object? That is not me. I have never seen a better mover than me. Man is attracted and threatened by difference. He kills the other out of jealousy, like the crazy Emperor Gao Yang (550-559A.D.), who chopped off courtesan Xue's head, dismembered her, and then used her thigh as the musical instrument *pipa* to bewail his love for her. I never kill the other; I depart from one to the next.

Perhaps I have defecated too much; a few sheets are spotted with nothing but yellow tears and red blood. I seem to have been purified, but purification is not necessarily a good thing. As the Chinese saying goes: If the water is pure, there is no fish; if a person is complete, he or she has no friends. Am I approaching a fearful completion or enclosure? I hope I will not be petrified into a bird-of-paradise flower who can never fly in spite of its yearnings.

Though I have wings
though I can fly
higher than a sparrow
almost out of sight
yet with an invisible string
to the ground I am tied—
soaring like an eagle
Nothing but a . . . .

I feel very hungry. I must be emaciated. Food, food—. Again, the old Chinese custom, a person should have a last fill of food before traveling to a different world. What do you want? Corn tortillas, tacos, pizza, hot dogs, cheeseburgers from McDonald's, salmon, rainbow trout, turkey. . . . Are you sure you do not want some Chinese food? I have had Chinese food all my life and I must take something different before I go.

Now I am staring at the large tray with the things I am craving. Among them, a Boston pear teases me to a chuckle. Two months ago, I gave Edna and Sam a basket of juicy pears as my present for their engagement party, a kind of present that can never make me feel regret or tip over my psychological balance. When I feel good about Edna and Sam, I would think in English and call my present "pear"—the auspicious wish of a permanent "pair." When I feel bad about Edna and Sam, I will think in Chinese and call my present "*li*"—a malicious omen of separation. East and West. *Li* and pear. *Li*—separation; pear—pair. Separation and pair; pair and separation. . . .

I continue to stare at the food of profusion of colors and shapes—staring is reading, and reading is eating. I eat and eat until I burp. When I close my eyes, I hear Mei crying. Don't cry. I am not dying yet. I will teach you some Chinese songs tomorrow.

A few drops fall on my face. Is the roof leaking again? Why, it smells like Long. Is Long shedding tears? He approaches me closer and closer. I can see his quivering lips. Do you still know how to kiss? We have not kissed each other for more than thirteen years—since the day we got married. I suddenly have a desire to kiss him. But today I am too exhausted. I will kiss you tomorrow. . . .